GFOA BUDGETING SERIES
Volume 3

Decision Tools
for
Budgetary Analysis

R. Gregory Michel

GOVERNMENT FINANCE OFFICERS ASSOCIATION

Copyright 2001 by the Government Finance Officers Association
of the United States and Canada
203 N. LaSalle Street, Suite 2700
Chicago, IL 60601-1210

ISBN no. 0-89125-251-7

LOC control number 2001 131427

Printed in the United States of America.

First printing, May 2001
Second printing, May 2002
Third printing, August 2004

Contents

EXHIBITS

Foreword

The finance officer of the information age faces complex decisions, but also has unprecedented access to data that, with the proper analysis tools, could be used to improve those decisions. To help the finance officer meet these challenges, this monograph describes 12 powerful analysis tools. This "toolbox" includes some basic tools, such as decision tables and decision trees, as well as several advanced tools, such as return on investment and cost-benefit analysis. The common characteristic of these tools is that they use a logical method that breaks a complex decision into manageable pieces.

To make these tools accessible to busy finance professionals, this monograph presents each tool in a concise way, focusing only on the essential elements of the tool. Each tool is given a brief description, a step-by-step procedure for using it, and an application specific to local government budgeting.

This publication is the third volume in the GFOA Budgeting Series that aids the implementation of the recommended practices of the National Advisory Council on State and Local Budgeting (NACSLB). Readers should find these tools most useful in the review/development phase of the budget process in which department budget requests are reviewed and resource allocation decisions are made. In the NACSLB budgeting framework, these analyses are found in Element 6, "Develop Programs and Services that are Consistent with Policies and Plans," and Element 9, "Develop and Evaluate Financial Options."

The GFOA would like to thank the author, R. Gregory Michel of the GFOA Research and Consulting Center, for writing this publication. We would also like to thank the reviewers for their insight and helpful comments: Drew S. Barden, City Economist, City of Portland, Oregon; Lisa L. Irvine, Director, Financial Management Department, City of San Diego, California; and Donald L. Rosdil, The University of Maryland. Thanks are also due to GFOA Director of Research and Consulting Rowan A. Miranda for his insightful comments.

Jeffrey L. Esser
Executive Director
Government Finance Officers Association

CHAPTER 1

Introduction

Government budgeting has entered a new era. Through the work of the National Advisory Council on State and Local Budgeting (NACSLB), governments now have a comprehensive set of practices defining a good budget process. The NACSLB's set of 59 practices is rapidly becoming the national standard for good budgeting. Through implementing these practices, governments are moving *away from* a budget process characterized by incrementalism, inefficient government programs, and a short-sightedness that puts them at risk of being blindsided by budget gaps, and *toward* a goal-oriented budget process in which programs are systematically evaluated for their performance, and financial decisions are made with a long-term view that greatly diminishes the risk of a fiscal emergency. To meet the standard of this new era of budgeting and tackle today's complex financial decisions, governments need to replace a "gut feeling" style of decision making with rigorous analytical tools.

The good news is that there are more resources available than ever before to help governments perform such analyses. Inexpensive computer hardware and software have greatly simplified and reduced the cost of sophisticated analysis. In addition, the World Wide Web and the CD-ROM media have dramatically cut the costs of information retrieval. Previously inaccessible financial and economic data can now be brought to any desktop computer—ready to be dropped into a spreadsheet. (See Appendix A for a list of Web data sources.)

This monograph presents 12 key decision tools and techniques to help budget analysts and managers meet the demands and opportunities of this new era of government budgeting. A decision tool is a specific, logical method of making a decision. The key feature of decision tools is their ability to cut a large, complex financial decision into many smaller, more manageable pieces. For example, instead of trying to consider all future costs and benefits of four alternatives *simultaneously,* the net present value decision tool directs the decision maker to consider the costs and benefits of a single alternative one year at a time—a much more manageable undertaking. Decision tools are useful for many types of financial decisions, including those related to: resource allocation, purchasing, capital programming, privatization, and land development.

If decision tools have a rival, their rival is the "gut feeling" method of making decisions. It has been argued that it is much easier and just as effective to make a "seat-of-the-pants" decision based on instinct rather than putting pencil to paper and using a decision tool. In fact, it is common practice to use an intuitive approach for many financial decisions. The reader should be warned, however, that the intuitive approach has several significant drawbacks.

One weakness of the intuitive approach is that it is highly dependent on a decision maker's personal experience. Because of this, a recent, unusual experience could bias a person's judgment and result in a bad decision. For example, a recent tornado could influence a decision maker to make excessive capital expenditures for safety equipment.

Another drawback of the intuitive approach is that the decision process occurs entirely in one person's mind, and thus cannot be evaluated by others. Decision tools, on the other hand, rely on an *explicit method*, allowing more than one person to evaluate the method and assumptions used to make a decision. This evaluation of assumptions by others is one way that a decision maker can avoid the bias of subjective experience.

The intuitive approach is also very susceptible to mistakes in which the intuitive answer is incorrect. Four of these intuitive pitfalls are:

- Failure to recognize the time value of money;
- Failure to recognize opportunity costs;
- Counting sunk costs; and,
- Cognitive illusions.

The *failure to recognize the time value of money* is the failure to recognize that a dollar today is worth more than a dollar tomorrow. *Failure to recognize opportunity costs* is the failure to quantify the lost opportunity of using an asset in a way other than the chosen alternative. *Counting sunk costs* refers to considering past, irreversible expenditures to justify a decision ("We should spend more on the project because we've already spent $X on the project").

Through a *cognitive illusion*, the human intuition can be tricked into misjudging the probability of an event. A cognitive illusion is much like an optical illusion. Believe it or not, the image below is not a spiral, but a series of concentric circles. The checkered background tricks visual perception by providing specific visual cues that normally would correctly identify a spiral.

Frazer spiral © 2001 IllusionWorks, L.L.C.

In the optical illusion above, the visual cues that would normally correctly identify a spiral cause us to misjudge the true character of this figure. In a *cognitive illusion*, the subconscious, intuitive methods that normally correctly estimate the probability of an event cause us to misjudge the probability of an event in particular instances. One subconscious, intuitive method that decision makers commonly use to estimate the probability of an event is to assign a probability to the event based on the ease with which it can be imagined. Generally, this technique can be a good method of estimating probability because events that occur more frequently (and thus have a higher probability) should come to mind easier. However, intuition can be tricked into overestimating the probability of an event when a similar, past event was very spectacular or recent. For example, travelers typically greatly overestimate the probability of being killed in an airplane crash (because it is very spectacular and can be remembered very easily), while they underestimate the probability of a car accident (because it is less spectacular).

Despite these drawbacks, decision makers may still rely on a gut feeling for some decisions because they perceive decision tools to be too complex and time-consuming. A goal of this book, then, is to make decision tools simple enough to use. Each tool's description is brief and focuses only on essential elements. Each description is followed by a step-by-step procedure on how to use the decision tool. Although entire books have been written to explain the nuances of just a single tool such as cost-benefit analysis, such a lengthy treatment often makes useful tools unreachable for many decision makers. This publication attempts to make useful decision tools more accessible to decision makers.

NACSLB's Recommended Budget Practices

The decision tools presented in this publication are important tools and techniques for accomplishing the following five NACSLB recommended practices:

> **Recommended Practice (RP) 6.1—Develop programs and evaluate delivery mechanisms:** *A government should develop programs and services that are consistent with policies and plans and should evaluate alternative delivery mechanisms.*

> **RP 6.2—Develop options for meeting capital needs and evaluate acquisition alternatives:** *A government should develop specific capital project options for addressing capital needs that are consistent with financial, programmatic, and capital policies and should evaluate alternatives for acquiring the use of capital assets.*

EXHIBIT 1-1 ■ **Using Decision Tools to Implement NACSLB Recommended Practices**

Budget Practice	Useful Tools
6.1–Develop programs and evaluate delivery mechanisms	• Decision table • Activity-based costing • Cost-effectiveness analysis
6.2–Develop options for meeting capital needs and evaluate acquisition alternatives	• Decision table • Net present value analysis • Cost-benefit analysis
9.4–Prepare expenditure projections	• Fiscal impact analysis • Sensitivity analysis
9.5–Evaluate revenue and expenditure options	• Sensitivity analysis
9.6–Develop a capital improvement plan	• Weighted score table • Decision tree • Net present value analysis • Return on investment analysis

RP 9.4—Prepare expenditure projections: *Governments should prepare multi-year projections of expenditures for each fund and for existing and proposed new programs.*

RP 9.5—Evaluate revenue and expenditure options: *A government should evaluate revenue and expenditure options together, and consider the implications for other financial indicators prior to making specific choices with regard to the proposed budget.*

RP 9.6—Develop a capital improvement plan: *A government should develop a capital improvement plan that identifies its priorities and time frame for undertaking capital projects and provides a financing plan for those projects.*

Exhibit 1-1 lists the tools that are useful for each practice.

ORGANIZATION OF THE BOOK

Following this introduction, Chapter 2 focuses on five basic decision tools that I call "hammers and wrenches." These tools are generally quick and simple to use. The tools covered in this chapter are:

- Decision tables;
- Expected value tables;
- Weighted score tables;
- Decision trees; and,
- Breakeven analysis.

Chapter 3 presents seven advanced decision tools that are the "jig saws and power lathes" of decision tools. These tools generally require more skill and time to use correctly. The tools introduced in this chapter are:

- Activity-based costing;
- Net present value analysis;
- Return on investment analysis;
- Cost-benefit analysis;
- Fiscal impact analysis;
- Cost-effectiveness analysis; and,
- Sensitivity analysis.

As a way of summarizing these 12 tools, Exhibit 1-2 lists seven of the most common types of budgetary decisions and provides a convenient guide to selecting the appropriate tool for each type of decision.

Chapter 4 introduces four techniques for simplifying decisions, and highlights some common pitfalls to avoid when it is necessary to make a seat-of-the-pants decision.

Chapter 5 shows how decision tools can help your government to accomplish five of the NACSLB's recommended practices.

Finally, Chapter 6 presents advice on how to communicate budgetary analysis to decision makers. This chapter focuses on the two most common forms of communication: memos and oral presentations.

EXHIBIT 1-2 ■ Selecting the Appropriate Decision Tool

In this type of decision...		*With these characteristics...*	*Choose this tool:*
Common Types of Budgetary Decisions	**Examples**	**Characteristics of the Decision**	**Appropriate Tools**
1. Financial planning	• Evaluating how changing future total revenue and expenditure levels will affect the government's financial condition.	• Revenue and expenditure levels and other assumptions could significantly affect the government's financial condition.	• Sensitivity Analysis
2. Resource allocation decisions (operating budget)	• Determining the best method of providing a government service • Deciding whether to privatize a city service • Deciding which government programs to fund • Deciding which government programs to cut	• Evaluating alternatives over a wide range of criteria. • Political, social, or other non-financial considerations are important.	• Decision Tables
		• Decisions in which the superiority of an alternative hinges on a future event that may or may not occur. • Evaluating alternatives that differ in price and quality.	• Expected Value Tables
		• Evaluating alternatives when criteria differ in importance.	• Weighted Score Tables
		• Decisions in which choosing a particular alternative leads to additional decisions with various future outcomes.	• Decision Trees
		• Determining the most efficient or effective alternative for providing a government service. • Decisions that are small in scope, with one primary benefit, and non-monetary costs can be ignored.	• Cost-Effectiveness Analysis
		• Decisions that could result in significant long-term financial costs or benefits.	• Net Present Value Analysis
		• Calculating the cost of a government service.	• Activity-based Costing
3. Setting tax rates and user fees	• Determining the user fee level that will cover the cost of a program.	• The benefits of the government service are narrow in scope and would be limited to those who pay the user fee.	• Activity-based Costing • Breakeven Analysis
	• Setting a tax rate to cover the cost of increased government expenditures due to a new residential development.	• The benefits of the government service are broad in scope with many beneficiaries.	• Fiscal Impact Analysis

EXHIBIT 1-2 (continued) ■ Selecting the Appropriate Decision Tool

In this type of decision...		*With these characteristics...*	*Choose this tool:*
Common Types of Budgetary Decisions	**Examples**	**Characteristics of the Decision**	**Appropriate Tools**
4. Deciding between proposed capital projects	• Constructing a parking garage • Constructing a public pool • Purchasing a fire engine	• Evaluating alternatives over a wide range of criteria. • Political, social, or other non-financial considerations are important.	• Decision Tables
		• Decisions in which the superiority of an alternative hinges on a future event that may or may not occur. • Evaluating alternatives that differ in price and quality.	• Expected Value Tables
		• Evaluating alternatives when criteria differ in importance.	• Weighted Score Tables
		• Decisions that could result in significant long-term financial costs or benefits. • Deciding between multiple projects.	• Net Present Value Analysis
	• Repair versus replacement decisions	• Decisions that could result in significant long-term financial costs or benefits. • Deciding between multiple projects.	• Net Present Value Analysis
	• Large scale capital projects such as incinerators, landfills, highways, major bridges	• Capital decisions that are very large in scope and generate important non-monetary costs and benefits. • Evaluating a single project.	• Cost-benefit Analysis
	• Testing whether a project breaks even over a broad range of discount rates	• Decisions that result in significant long term costs or benefits. • Evaluating a single project.	• Return on Investment Analysis
		• Determining the effect that changes in key assumptions would have on the recommendation of a decision tool.	• Sensitivity Analysis

EXHIBIT 1-2 (continued) ■ Selecting the Appropriate Decision Tool

In this type of decision...		With these characteristics...	Choose this tool:
Common Types of Budgetary Decisions	**Examples**	**Characteristics of the Decision**	**Appropriate Tools**
5. Determining the best use of a capital asset	• Deciding the best use of vacant government property or facilities.	• Evaluating alternatives over a wide range of criteria. • Political, social, or other non-financial considerations are important.	• Decision Tables
		• Evaluating alternatives when criteria differ in importance.	• Weighted Score Tables
		• Decisions that could result in significant long-term financial costs or benefits. • Deciding between multiple projects.	• Net Present Value Analysis
6. Determining the impact of economic development	• Residential subdivision development • Rezoning • Annexation • Business tax incentive program • Shopping mall	• Estimating impact on governmental expenditures and revenues. • Decisions in which the overriding consideration is the financial costs and benefits to the government.	• Fiscal Impact Analysis
		• Estimating total societal impact • Capital decisions that are very large in scope and generate important non-monetary costs and benefits. • Evaluating a single project.	• Cost-benefit Analysis
7. Determining the financing method with the lowest cost	• Deciding between pay-as-you-go and debt financing • Lease-purchase decisions	• Decisions that could result in significant long-term financial costs or benefits.	• Net Present Value Analysis

CHAPTER 2

Basic Decision Tools

The five decision tools described in this chapter are the "hammers and wrenches" of decision tools. Most are quick and simple to use. These tools can be used alone or as "accessories" of more sophisticated tools. For example, expected value tables can be used to provide the data necessary to use the net present value analysis tool, while decision tables can be used to compare the data from a net present value analysis with political and social considerations.

The tools in this chapter are most useful in the review/development phase of the budget process, in which department budget requests are reviewed and resource allocation decisions are made. In the National Advisory Council on State and Local Budgeting (NACSLB) framework, these decisions are found in Element 6, "Develop Programs and Services that are Consistent with Policies and Plans," and Element 9, "Develop and Evaluate Financial Options." Four of the tools provide methods of comparing alternatives: decision tables, expected value tables, weighted score tables, and decision trees. Breakeven analysis provides a simple technique to evaluate whether a program is self-supporting.

TOOL 1: DECISION TABLES

A decision table is a useful method of organizing the key information in a decision. In a decision table, each alternative is represented by a separate column and each criterion or requirement is given a separate row.

EXHIBIT 2-1 ▪ A Decision Table

Criteria	Alternatives		
	In-house	Privatize	County
Cost	$300,000	$700,000	$450,000
Quality	Satisfactory	Good	Poor
Average Turnaround	5 hours	1 hour	2 hours

The cells in each column represent an alternative's value or score for each criterion.

Exhibit 2-1 shows a simple decision table that might be used to decide between three alternatives for providing printing services for a city government. The city's budget director uses this table to compare three alternatives:

- Providing the printing services in-house through the Bureau of General Services;
- Privatizing the printing function; and,
- Having the county government provide the services through an intergovernmental agreement.

The three alternatives differ in price, quality, and average turnaround time. A decision table provides a method of comparing the strengths and weaknesses of each alternative.

The primary advantage of decision tables is that they help an analyst to organize and consider the key information in a decision. Decision tables force an analyst to specify all of the important criteria in a decision and the possible alternatives, and to consider each alternative's score or value for each criterion. Decision tables also make it easy to compare many alternatives. If scores are given to each alternative for each criterion, a decision table can be used to calculate and display a total score for each alternative.

Limitations of Tool

One limitation of decision tables is that they assume that a single number or score can capture an alternative's value for a criterion. For example, in a decision table, the cost of a new public parking garage would be represented by a single number, when the actual cost would be a *stream* of costs over time. In other words, a decision table provides a "snapshot" view of alternatives when, in some cases, a "camcorder" is needed. (Decision tools 7 and 8, net present value analysis and return on investment analysis, provide this "camcorder" view.) A snapshot view of alternatives is also inadequate when alternatives could have more than one outcome. The next decision tool, expected value tables, provides a method of evaluating this type of uncertainty.

Another limitation of decision tables is that they merely organize the information in a decision; they do not indicate which alternative is the best. However, this limitation also makes decision tables the most versatile of all of the tools in this book. Unlike many of the other tools, decision tables can be an effective tool in decisions where political, social, or other non-financial considerations are critical.

TOOL 2: EXPECTED VALUE TABLES

Expected value is simply a method of weighting the result of a scenario by the probability of the scenario—for example, weighting the cost of fixing a broken water pump by the probability that it will break. This tool is most useful for deciding between two items that differ in price and quality. Expected value makes this comparison possible by weighting the initial price of an item by its quality.

To see how the expected value tool can be useful, suppose a city is deciding between two river dike projects. The "high dike" proposal costs $2.5 million and will protect the city against a ten-foot rise in the river. The "low dike" proposal costs $1.4 million and will protect the city against a five-foot rise in the river. Proponents of the high dike argue that the additional cost is worth the additional security that the dike will provide the city. So which proposal is better? Expected value provides a method to answer this question.

Exhibit 2-2 uses an expected value table to determine which dike is a better value. The first column lists the two alternatives, high dike and low dike. The second column lists the possible future scenarios, and the third column lists the probability of each scenario. The outcome (or net benefit) in each scenario is estimated in the fourth column. The outcome in a normal scenario is the cost of constructing the dike. The outcome in a major flood scenario is the cost of constructing the dike plus the cost of property damage if the dike fails. To calculate the weighted outcomes in

EXHIBIT 2-2 ■ An Expected Value Table

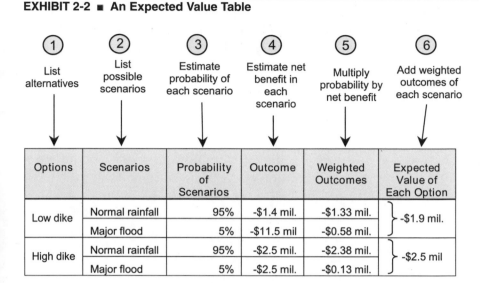

Options	Scenarios	Probability of Scenarios	Outcome	Weighted Outcomes	Expected Value of Each Option
Low dike	Normal rainfall	95%	-$1.4 mil.	-$1.33 mil.	-$1.9 mil.
	Major flood	5%	-$11.5 mil	-$0.58 mil.	
High dike	Normal rainfall	95%	-$2.5 mil.	-$2.38 mil.	-$2.5 mil
	Major flood	5%	-$2.5 mil.	-$0.13 mil.	

the fifth column, the outcome in each scenario is multiplied by the probability of that scenario. Finally, to calculate an expected value of each dike, the weighted outcomes of every scenario are summed. This exhibit shows that the low dike is the better value because it has the highest expected value: –$1.9 million.

It is important to realize that this expected value of –$1.9 million is a *weighted* number, not an *actual* number. That is, the government will never pay this amount. It will either pay $1.4 million in a normal scenario or $11.5 million in a major flood. Although the expected value of –$1.9 million is not an actual number, it is still very useful because it reflects:

- The initial cost of the dike;
- The probability of the dike failing; and,
- The cost if the dike fails.

In other words, by calculating the expected value, it is possible to compare two items that differ in price and quality because the expected value reflects *both* the price and quality.

Limitations of Tool

The primary limitation of this tool is that many times it is difficult to accurately determine the probability of a future outcome. This is a serious weakness that limits this tool to decisions in which reliable probability data is available, or to decisions in which less precision is necessary because there is a large difference in the probability of future outcomes.

TOOL 3: WEIGHTED SCORE TABLES

The criteria in most decisions are usually not of equal importance. For example, in purchasing a drinking water filtration system, reliability may be a more important criterion than price. A weighted score table is an effective way to evaluate alternatives when criteria differ in importance.

In a weighted score table, each alternative is given a score for each criterion. These scores are then weighted by the importance of each criterion. All of an alternative's weighted scores are then added together to calculate that alternative's total weighted score. The alternative with the highest total score should be the best alternative.

To complete a weighted score table, list each criterion in the first column and assign weights to each criterion in the second column. Weight each criterion on a scale of 1 percent to 100 percent (0.01 to 1.00), with 100 percent being the highest possible importance. List alternatives as additional columns in the table. Give each alternative a score, on a scale of 1 to 10, for each of the criteria. Multiply each of the scores by the weight of the criterion to calculate a weighted score. Sum each alternative's weighted scores to calculate that alternative's total weighted score. The alternative with the highest total weighted score should be the best alternative. Exhibit 2-3 illustrates these steps.

In this example, none of the alternatives stand out as superior for all of the criteria. Fire engine A has mediocre scores for all three criteria. Fire engines B and C have high scores for one criterion, but lower scores for the other criteria. By calculating a weighted score, however, it becomes apparent that fire engine A is the best alternative.

Limitations of Tool

One limitation of this tool is the difficulty in assigning a numerical score for non-quantitative criteria, such as conformance to city goals, political

EXHIBIT 2-3 ■ A Weighted Score Table

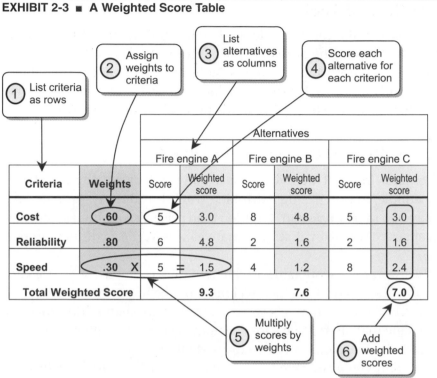

acceptance, resident satisfaction, etc. Another limitation of this tool is that the scoring and weighting is subjective in nature and subject to manipulation. For example, if a particular alternative is preferred, its scores might be inflated or a particular criterion might be weighted highly to favor the alternative. One method of avoiding this bias is to weight criteria before scores are given. Another method is to assign different individuals the tasks of scoring alternatives and weighting criteria.

TOOL 4: DECISION TREES

A decision tree represents a decision in a graphical form. Decision trees are particularly useful for complex decisions where choosing a particular alternative could lead to several possible outcomes, and those outcomes to future decisions. Unless you are a master at chess, it is difficult to consider a series of future decisions that you may have to make if you

EXHIBIT 2-4 ■ A Decision Tree

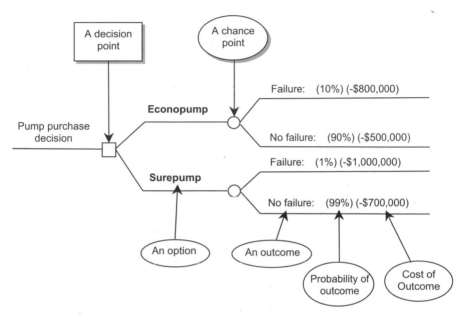

select a certain alternative today. As with long division, decision trees make it easy to do on paper that which is difficult to do in your head.

A decision tree diagrams a decision by representing each alternative as a separate branch. Additional branches extending from the branch of each alternative represent possible future outcomes. The branch for each outcome lists the probability and the payoff associated with that outcome. A choice between multiple options is represented by a square in the decision tree. A circle in the decision tree represents a point where more than one outcome could occur based on chance. Exhibit 2-4 shows a simple decision tree.

Determining the Best Alternative by Calculating the Expected Value

Decision trees determine the best alternative by calculating each alternative's expected value. As mentioned earlier, expected value is a method of weighting the cost or benefit of an outcome by the probability of the outcome. Exhibit 2-5 shows how to calculate the expected cost of Econopump. There are three steps. First, the cost of Econopump with a failure ($800,000) is weighted by the probability of a failure (10 per-

EXHIBIT 2-5 ▪ Calculating the Expected Value in a Decision Tree

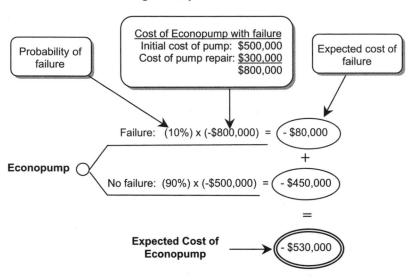

cent) to calculate the expected cost of a failure ($80,000). (The cost of a failure is the initial cost of the pump, $500,000, plus the cost of repairing the pump, $300,000.) Second, the cost of Econopump in a no-failure scenario is also weighted by the probability of a no-failure scenario to get an expected cost of $450,000. Third, the expected costs in both scenarios are added together to calculate the expected cost of Econopump ($530,000).

One of the strengths of decision trees is that they make it relatively easy to consider the future consequences of a decision. The decision tree in Exhibit 2-6 illustrates a decision in which the outcomes of selecting Pump A result in a future decision with additional alternatives and outcomes.

Steps to Using Decision Trees

There are nine basic steps to using a decision tree.

1. Draw one branch for each main alternative.
2. If an alternative has variations, list these as additional branches coming out of the alternative.
3. For each alternative, list a separate branch for each possible outcome.
4. Determine the probability of each outcome and write it on the appropriate branch.

EXHIBIT 2-6 ■ **A Decision Tree in Which Selecting an Alternative Leads to a Future Decision**

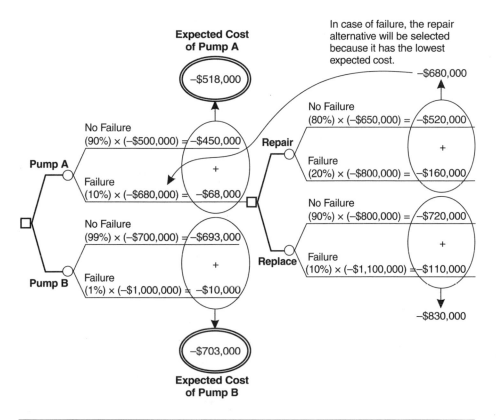

5. If possible, determine the final net benefit (benefit-cost) of each outcome and write it on the appropriate branch.

6. If it is not possible to determine the final net benefit because the final outcome is dependent on the outcome of additional decisions, draw each additional decision as a separate branch and repeat steps 1 to 5.

7. Calculate the expected net benefit of each major alternative. Beginning at the end of the branch of each alternative, multiply the probability of each outcome by the net benefit of each outcome to calculate the expected benefit of each outcome. For each alternative, sum the expected benefits of each of the alternative's outcomes to calculate the expected benefit of that alternative.

8. Select the alternative with the highest expected benefit.

Limitations of Tool

Decision tables share the same limitations as expected value tables, namely, the difficulty of accurately determining the probability of future outcomes. Another limitation of decision trees is that they can become cumbersome to use if a decision has an excessive number of alternatives and contingencies.

TOOL 5: BREAK-EVEN ANALYSIS

Break-even analysis is a simple technique for determining whether a project will break even (i.e., for the revenues to equal the costs). The main component of this tool is the following formula:

Break-even Formula for a Service

$$\text{Break-even number of users} = \frac{\text{Fixed cost}}{(\text{Revenue per user} - \text{Variable cost per user})}$$

Put into words, this formula states that a project will break even when the number of users is equal to the project's fixed costs divided by the revenue gained per user minus the variable cost per user. Since governments are in the people business, the break-even formula will likely be written in terms of *number of users* or *visits*. If a product is being produced, however, this formula can also be written in the following way:

Break-even Formula for a Product

$$\text{Break-even quantity} = \frac{\text{Fixed cost}}{(\text{Revenue per unit} - \text{Variable cost per unit})}$$

Fixed and Variable Costs

To use break-even analysis, it is important to understand fixed and variable costs. A *fixed cost* remains the same when the number of users or units increases or decreases. An example of a fixed cost for a city's paramedic service[1] is the cost of maintaining the fire station. The mainte-

---

1. This example does not suggest that break-even analysis should be used to determine a user fee for a paramedic service. Break-even analysis is not a good tool for evaluating a government service such as a paramedic service because the break-even formula does not capture the full benefit that residents obtain from the service. The break-even formula only considers the benefit of those who are treated by the paramedics. The citizens in the community (who are not treated) also receive a significant benefit by having this service available if they need it.

EXHIBIT 2-7 ■ **A Comparison of Fixed and Variable Costs**

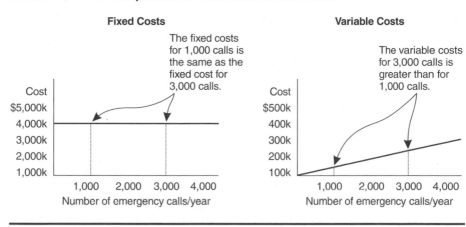

nance cost of the fire station will remain the same regardless of the number of emergency calls that the city receives. A *variable cost* changes proportionally as the number of users or units increases or decreases. An example of a variable cost for the city's paramedic service is fuel costs, which will increase proportionately with the number of emergency calls. Exhibit 2-7 shows fixed and variable costs in a graphical way. As the number of emergency calls increases, the paramedic service's fixed costs remain at $4 million. However, the service's variable costs increase as the number of emergency calls increases.

An important consideration when calculating fixed and variable costs is the time horizon of the analysis. Whether a cost is defined as *fixed* or *variable* depends on the time horizon. For example, if the time horizon is a year, personnel costs will be defined as a fixed cost.[2] The number of paramedics is unlikely to change as the number of calls changes from day to day. However, if the time horizon is ten years, then personnel costs will be defined as a variable cost. A government is likely to hire more paramedics if the average number of calls increases significantly on an annual basis.

To illustrate how to use break-even analysis, suppose a town government is determining whether a proposed public pool will break even. The estimated fixed cost of the facility will be $100,000 per year, the variable cost is $0.30 per visit, the pool will charge $1.50 per visit,

---

2. This assumes that the paramedics are salaried employees. If the paramedics can work overtime, personnel costs would be a variable cost.

and the estimated number of visits per year is 50,000. The calculation below shows that the pool will break even at 83,333 visits, 33,333 short of the expected number of visits.

$$\frac{83,333}{\text{visits}} = \frac{\$100,000}{(\$1.50 - \$0.30)}$$

The break-even formula can be quite useful. If three of the four variables are known, this formula can be rewritten to solve for any one of the four variables. For example, the break-even formula could be used to solve for the revenue per unit. This would be useful if a county wanted to determine the fee that it should charge in order for its building inspection program to break even. To perform this analysis, the first step would be to rearrange the break-even formula by solving the equation for the revenue per unit:

Calculating the Fee Necessary to Break Even

$$\frac{\text{Revenue}}{\text{per unit}} = \left(\frac{\text{Fixed cost}}{\text{Number of units}}\right) + \left(\begin{array}{c}\text{Variable}\\\text{cost per}\\\text{unit}\end{array}\right)$$

If a county's building inspection program currently has fixed costs of $300,000 per year, total variable costs of $70,000, and conducts an average of 4,000 building inspections per year, then it would use the formula below to calculate the user fee that it would have to charge for the program to break even. The variable cost per unit would be the total variable cost divided by the number of building inspections ($70,000 ÷ 4,000 = $17.50 per building inspection).

$$\begin{array}{c}\$92.50\\\text{per building}\\\text{inspection}\end{array} = \left(\frac{\$300,000}{4,000}\right) + \left(\begin{array}{c}\$17.50\\\text{per}\\\text{inspection}\end{array}\right)$$

This calculation shows that the county would have to charge a user fee of $92.50 per building inspection in order to break even.

Limitations of Tool

Break-even analysis has several significant limitations that should be noted. First, the analysis is valid for a limited range of users or units. As the number of users/units becomes much larger or smaller, the fixed and variable costs may change. Second, break-even analysis ignores the time value of money. The time value of money is the concept that a dollar today is worth more than a dollar tomorrow. (This concept will be discussed in decision tool 7, net present value analysis). Third, it may be difficult to obtain accurate estimates of fixed and variable costs.

CHAPTER 3

Advanced Decision Tools

The tools introduced in this chapter are the "jig saws and power lathes" of decision tools. Jig saws and power lathes are sophisticated tools that require skill and experience to use correctly. In the same way, the tools introduced in this chapter—cost-benefit analysis, fiscal impact analysis, net present value analysis, etc.—require more skill than the tools introduced in the previous chapter. The reader should note that this chapter does not attempt to provide a comprehensive discussion of each tool. However, the reader should gain a general understanding of each tool and how to use it.

As with the tools in chapter two, the tools in this chapter are most useful in the review/development phase of the budget process. Activity-based costing is a method of estimating the total costs of a government service. Cost data from this method can be used to determine whether private suppliers could deliver a service more efficiently. Net present value analysis and cost effectiveness analysis are tools that can be used to evaluate competing alternatives. Cost-benefit analysis, fiscal impact analysis, and return on investment analysis are useful tools to evaluate the merits of a *single* alternative. Sensitivity analysis is a tool that can be used to test how sensitive an analysis is to changes in the underlying assumptions.

EXHIBIT 3-1 ■ **Estimating the Cost of a Support Activity with a Cost Driver**

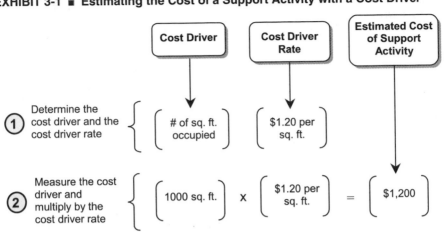

TOOL: 6: ACTIVITY-BASED COSTING

Activity-based costing (ABC) is a method of estimating the total costs of a government service, including the direct costs of labor and materials *and* the indirect costs of support activities. ABC isolates the indirect costs of a government service by first dividing the government into many discrete activities or support services, such as utility usage, mail service, facility maintenance, finance and administration, insurance, and so forth. For each of these support services a *cost driver* is determined. A cost driver is a measure of how much a support service is being used. Cost drivers should be closely correlated with the cost of the support service. An example of a cost driver for a finance department's utility usage might be the *square footage of office space occupied,* because the cost of the utilities will increase in direct proportion to the square footage occupied. A cost driver is used because it is easier to measure than the cost of the support activity for a specific program. For example, it is easier to measure the square footage occupied by the finance department than the electricity and gas costs of the finance department. If the relationship between the cost driver and the cost is known, then the actual costs can be estimated by measuring the cost driver.

Exhibit 3-1 shows how a cost driver estimates the utility usage costs of a finance department. The cost driver that is used is the square footage of office space occupied. The cost driver rate is calculated to be $1.20 per square foot (per year). (The cost driver rate shows the relation-

EXHIBIT 3-2 ■ **How ABC Estimates the Direct and Indirect Costs of a Government Service**

Table 1

Costs and Rates for All Government Services

Activity	Total Annual Cost	Cost Driver	Total Cost Driver Level	Cost Driver Rate
Vehicle maintenance	$100,000	Garage labor hours	720 hrs.	$139/hr.
Vehicle insurance	$60,000	Mileage/ year	400,000 miles	$0.15/mile
Utility usage	$2,400	Square ft. occupied	2,000 sq. ft.	$1.20 sq. ft.
Facility maintenance	$6,000	Square ft. occupied	2,000 sq. ft.	$3 sq. ft.
Payroll processing	$20,000	# of employees	200 employees	$100/ employee

> **Stage 1**
> Calculate the cost driver rate of each activity based on all government services.

Table 2

Cost of Street Cleaning Services

Direct Labor Costs

Employees	Hours	Wage/hr.	Cost
Driver	800	$10/ hr.	$8,000

Direct Material Costs

Material	Amount	Cost/unit	Cost
Fuel	1000 gal.	$1.50/ gal.	$1,500

Indirect Support Costs

Activity	Cost Driver Level	Cost Driver Rate	Cost
Vehicle maintenance	5 hrs.	$139/hr.	$695
Vehicle insurance	10,000 miles	$0.15/mile	$1,500
Utility usage	120 sq. ft.	$1.20 sq. ft.	$144
Facility maintenance	120 sq. ft.	$3 sq. ft.	$360
Payroll processing	1 employee	$100/ employee	$100

TOTAL ANNUAL COST: **$12,299**

> **Stage 2**
> Calculate the total cost of a specific government service using the cost driver rates from stage 1.

ship between the cost driver and the actual cost.) Multiplying the cost driver level (1,000 square feet) by the cost driver rate will yield the estimated cost of this support activity for the finance department.

Exhibit 3-2 illustrates how to use ABC to estimate the total costs of street cleaning services. In Table 1, all of the government's activities are listed in the first column, and the cost of each activity is listed in the second column. (This is the total cost of the activity for all government services.) The third column lists cost drivers for each activity. The level of each cost driver (for all government services) is recorded in the fourth column. An average rate for each cost driver is calculated by dividing the cost of each activity by its cost driver rate.

Table 2 calculates the total costs of a specific government service using the cost driver rates from the first table. The total cost is the sum of the direct costs for labor and materials and the indirect costs of support activities. The indirect costs of support activities are calculated by measuring the cost driver levels for each activity and multiplying this by each activity's cost driver rate.

ABC and Conventional Two-Stage Costing Systems

ABC is different from conventional two-stage costing systems in the way that it estimates indirect support costs. ABC ties the cost that is estimated for a support activity *directly* to a government service's use of the activity. Conventional two-stage costing systems, however, add another step that disassociates the cost that is estimated for a support activity from the government service's use of the activity. Conventional two-stage costing systems first estimate an *entire department's* use of support services, and then estimate a government service's proportion of the department's costs. A distortion can occur when a service's proportion of the department's cost is significantly different from its proportional use of the support activity.

Exhibit 3-3 illustrates how conventional two-stage costing systems can overestimate or underestimate indirect support costs, and how ABC avoids this distortion. In this example, a city wants to compare the annual operating costs of two fire stations. Both stations are within the fire department and have vehicles serviced by the public works department (which also services the city's entire fleet of vehicles). While station one has typical fire fighting equipment, station two has specialized equipment that can be used for hazardous chemical fires. Both stations

EXHIBIT 3-3 ■ Two Methods of Estimating Support Costs

> **Conventional Two-Stage Costing System**

1. Allocate a portion of the support costs for vehicle maintenance, payroll processing and vehicle insurance to the fire department.

	A	B	C	(A ÷ B) × C
Activity	**Cost driver level for *fire* dept. (e.g., # of work orders for fire dept. vehicles)**	**Cost driver level for *entire* city (e.g., hours maintaining all city vehicles)**	**Support cost for entire city (e.g., cost of maintaining all city vehicles)**	**Support cost allocated to fire dept. (e.g., cost of maintaining fire dept. vehicles)**
Vehicle maintenance	130 work orders	1,500 work orders	$350,000	$30,333
Facility maintenance	8,751 sq. ft.	300,000 sq. ft.	$700,000	$20,000
Finance & administration	70 employees	500 employees	$7,000,000	$980,000
			Total support costs allocated to fire department:	$1,030,333

2. Determine the average cost per fire department call.

A	B	A ÷ B
Total support costs of fire department	**Total fire dept. calls**	**Average cost per fire dept. call**
$1,030,333	500 calls	$2,061/call

3. Allocate a portion of the fire department's costs to each station based on the intensity of each station's activity (as measured by the number of calls responded to).

	A	B	A × B
	Calls per year	**Average cost per fire dept. call**	**Total support cost of station**
Station One	30	$2,061/call	$61,830
Station Two	30	$2,061/call	$61,830

> A conventional costing system incorrectly assigns the same support costs to both stations

EXHIBIT 3-3 (continued) ■ **Two Methods of Estimating Support Costs**

> **Activity-Based Costing**

1. Calculate the cost driver rate for each activity.

	A	B	A ÷ B
Activity	**Total Cost**	**Cost driver level**	**Cost driver rate**
Vehicle maintenance	$350,000	1,500 work orders	$233/work order
Facility maintenance	$700,000	300,000 sq.ft.	$2.33/sq.ft.
Finance & administration	$7,000,000	500 employees	$14,000/employee

2. For each station, multiply the cost driver level by the cost driver rate of each activity.

Station One

	A	B	A x B
Activity	**Cost driver level**	**Cost driver rate**	**Cost**
Vehicle maintenance	4 work orders	$233/work order	$932
Facility maintenance	1,000 sq. ft.	$2.33/sq.ft.	$2,330
Finance & administration	4 employees	$14,000/employee	$56,000
		Total support cost:	$59,262

Station Two

	A	B	A x B
Activity	**Cost driver level**	**Cost driver rate**	**Cost**
Vehicle maintenance	30 work orders	$233/work order	$6,990
Facility maintenance	1,000 sq. ft.	$2.33/sq.ft.	$2,330
Finance & administration	4 employees	$14,000/employee	$56,000
		Total support cost:	$65,320

> ABC recognizes that station two has higher vehicle maintenance costs

spend the same amount of time fighting fires, but station two's specialized equipment has vehicle maintenance costs that are three times higher than those of station one. The example shows that a conventional two-stage costing system underestimates the costs of station two because it does not allocate vehicle maintenance costs directly to each station. Instead, vehicle maintenance and other support service costs are allocated to the entire fire department. Each station is then allocated a portion of the department's support costs based on the intensity of each station's activity (measured by number of calls responded to). ABC correctly estimates the costs of both trucks because it allocates vehicle maintenance costs based on each station's use of this support service.

Limitations of Tool

The key drawback of ABC is the difficulty of defining good cost drivers and setting up the account structure necessary to collect cost data on activities. Defining good cost drivers requires knowledge of the factors that influence the costs of support activities. Setting up an account structure to collect ABC data can be a major, organization-wide undertaking.

TOOL 7: NET PRESENT VALUE ANALYSIS

Net present value analysis is a method of comparing the long-term, financial costs and benefits of different alternatives. This method converts an alternative's stream of future costs and benefits into a single number—its net present value. Once all of the benefits and costs of each alternative are converted into a single number, a decision maker can easily compare the alternatives and select the alternative with the highest value or least cost.

The net present value tool generates a single number by converting an alternative's future benefits and costs into their value as if they were given today. The process of converting a future value into the value it would be given today is called *discounting*. This process of discounting is the outstanding feature of the net present value tool. Discounting is necessary because a dollar in the future is not worth the same as a dollar today. Investing is a good way to illustrate this concept. Suppose a person is given a choice between receiving $100 today and a promise to receive $100 five years in the future. The promise to receive $100 five years in the future is worse than receiving $100 today for several reasons:

- The person giving the money may not be able to fulfill his promise in five years;
- The $100 given five years in the future could have been invested and increased in value if it was given earlier;
- Inflation may reduce the value of $100 five years from today; and,
- If the $100 were given earlier, it could have been spent on necessary expenses.

Obviously, the promise to receive $100 five years in the future is worth less than $100 today. But how much less? Discounting provides a method of calculating this. Discounting converts a future value into a present value by dividing the future value by a number called a *discount factor*. The discount factor captures the effect that time has in reducing a future value.

$$\frac{(\$100 \text{ promised in future})}{(\text{Discount factor})} = (\text{The value of the promise today})$$

To calculate the discount factor in this example we need two pieces of information: (1) the number of years until the money will be given, and (2) the interest rate that could be earned if the money was received today and invested. In this example, the money will be given in five years and the interest rate is 5 percent. To calculate the discount factor, we simply plug these two numbers into the formula below:

$$\text{Discount factor} = (\text{Interest rate} + 1)^{\text{number of years}}$$

$$1.276 = (0.05 + 1)^5$$

Finally, to calculate the value of the promise today, we can simply divide the $100 promise by our discount factor of 1.276.

$$\text{Value of the promise today} = \frac{(\$100 \text{ promised in future})}{(\text{Discount factor})} = \frac{\$100}{1.276} = \$78.37$$

So, the promise of receiving $100 in five years is equal to receiving $78.37 today. The formula to calculate the present value of a future amount of money is:

$$\text{Present value} = \frac{(\text{Amount promised in future})}{(\text{Interest rate} + 1)^{\# \text{ of years until received}}}$$

In this formula, the interest rate is also known as the *discount rate*. A discount rate is like an exchange rate that converts dollars in the future to dollars today. In the example above, the discount rate was the interest rate that could be earned if the $100 was invested. For many decisions, however, the discount rate is not the interest rate on an investment, but another number that reflects a government's cost of borrowing or a community's preference for present versus future consumption. Step 2 below will discuss how to determine a discount rate.

How To Do a Net Present Value Analysis

Net present value analysis involves five basic steps. The first step is to forecast the benefits and costs in each year. The second step is to determine a discount rate. The third step is to use a formula to calculate the net present value. The fourth step is to compare the net present values of the alternatives. The final step is to determine whether the alternative with the highest net present value is fundable.

Step 1: For Each Alternative, Forecast the Benefits and Costs in Each Year

Forecast the total benefits and total costs in each year. A typical forecast of costs and benefits might look something like this:

		Year									
	Now	1	2	3	4	5	6	7	8	9	10
Benefits	$0	$32	$47	$47	$47	$47	$47	$47	$47	$47	$500
Costs	–$950	–$40	–$5	–$5	–$5	–$5	–$5	–$65	–$5	–$5	–$5

Making accurate forecasts of future costs and benefits can be the most difficult step in net present value analysis. Analysts should follow five general rules when forecasting costs and benefits.
1. Forecast benefits and costs in today's dollars.
2. Do not include sunk costs.
3. Include opportunity costs.
4. Use expected value to estimate uncertain benefits and costs.
5. Omit non-monetary costs and benefits.

Forecast benefits and costs in today's dollars. It is important to treat inflation consistently throughout a net present value calculation, so all forecasts of future costs and benefits should be made in today's dollars, i.e., *real* dollars, and discounted at a *real* discount rate.[1] When a forecast is made in real dollars, future costs and benefits are not increased to include the effect of inflation. In other words, if a benefit of $100,000 is forecast for the fifth year of a project, that $100,000 will have the same buying power as $100,000 today.

As an alternative to making forecasts in real dollars, it is also possible to make all forecasts in nominal dollars and discount them at a nominal discount rate. However, it can be argued that forecasts in real dollars are easier to make and understand than forecasts in nominal dollars. It is easier to make forecasts in real dollars because inflation does not complicate the forecast. For example, if an analyst forecasts the future revenues of a swimming pool in *nominal* dollars, the forecast for each year must take into account both the number of users of the pool *and* the effect of inflation. If the same forecast is made in *real* dollars, only the number of users (or real increase in revenue) needs to be projected. It is also easier to understand forecasts in real dollars. Excluding inflation from the forecast makes it clear that an increase in costs or benefits is an actual increase, and not simply an increase due to inflation.[2]

Do not include sunk costs. A sunk cost is one that has already occurred and will remain the same regardless of what decision is made. An example of a sunk cost is the cost of conducting a survey to determine resident interest in an outdoor pool. The cost of the survey is a sunk cost because it will remain the same regardless whether a pool is built.

To see how including sunk costs can lead to bad decisions, suppose a county government is considering demolishing its 52-year-old high

---

1. It is also possible to make all forecasts in nominal dollars and discount them at a nominal discount rate. In either case, inflation should be treated consistently.
2. There are also advantages to making forecasts in nominal dollars and using a nominal discount rate. If a forecast is made in nominal dollars, the analyst knows the actual number of dollars that will be spent or received each year. This is important for budgeting and financing decisions. Forecasts in nominal dollars also make it easier to recalculate the analysis at a future date because the forecasts are made in terms of the value of a dollar in each year rather than the value of a dollar in the year that the analysis was made. Finally, nominal discount rates can be easily compared to other governments that use nominal discount rates.

school and building a new facility on the same site. One year earlier, the county had spent $1.2 million to meet an EPA deadline for asbestos removal. Opponents of the new facility argue that the old building shouldn't be abandoned since the county had just poured $1.2 million into it to bring it into compliance with EPA regulations. However, this argument could justify renovating the building forever since each new renovation could be justified by the money that has been "invested" in the building already. The $1.2 million for asbestos removal is a sunk cost and should be ignored because it cannot be recovered regardless of the decision that is made. If the cost of renovating and expanding the old building is $4.3 million and the cost of demolishing the old building and building a new facility is $3.4 million, the county would save $900,000 by selecting a new facility. In other words, including the sunk cost of the asbestos removal would lead the county to spend $900,000 more than it has to for a high school facility.

Include opportunity costs. When forecasting costs, it is important to include opportunity costs. The opportunity costs of a proposed project are the potential benefits that are lost by selecting it. For example, if a city decides to build a public pool on vacant city-owned property, the city would lose the potential revenue it would generate by selling the land to a developer. This potential revenue is the opportunity cost of the pool, and it should be included as a cost of the pool.

If opportunity costs are not included as costs, then some proposals may appear to be better just because they use existing government resources. To show how this can lead to bad decisions, suppose a small city government is considering two proposals for a community center. The first proposal would involve use of a vacant, downtown, city-owned building (one that could be sold for $2.3 million). The second proposal would require the purchase of vacant land in a residential area. The top box in Exhibit 3-4 illustrates what the costs and benefits of both proposals would look like in the first year if the opportunity cost of using the city building were ignored.

Note that the total cost of proposal A ($0.7 million) appears to be $1 million less than the total cost of proposal B ($1.7 million). The bottom box in Exhibit 3-4 illustrates what the costs and benefits look like when the opportunity cost is included.

Since the building could be sold for $2.3 million, its value to the city government is $2.3 million. Therefore, using this building for a commu-

EXHIBIT 3-4 ■ Including vs. Ignoring Opportunity Cost

Ignoring Opportunity Cost	
Proposal A – Use City Building	**Proposal B – Purchase Land**
Land purchase cost $0 Construction cost $0.7 m Total Cost $0.7 m	Land purchase cost $0.5 m Construction cost $1.2 m Total Cost $1.7 m

Including Opportunity Cost	
Proposal A – Use City Building	**Proposal B – Purchase Land**
Opportunity cost of ($2.3 m) city building Construction cost $0.7 m Total Cost $3.0 m	Land purchase cost $0.5 m Construction cost $1.2 m Total Cost $1.7 m

nity center entails an opportunity cost of $2.3 million. Including this opportunity cost shows that the total cost of proposal A is $1.3 million *more* than proposal B.

To discover opportunity costs, first consider all of the government resources that are used by the proposed project—land, employee time, facilities, etc. Second, determine the value of each of these resources to the government, or the greatest benefit that the government would obtain by using each resource in another way. Record this benefit as a cost of the proposal.

Use expected value to estimate uncertain benefits and costs. Many times it is difficult to estimate the benefits or costs because they are dependent on an unpredictable environment or because the result of a project is uncertain. However, it is still possible to make an estimate by using the following technique:

1. List the possible scenarios.
2. Estimate the probability of each scenario.
3. Estimate the benefit (or cost) in each scenario.
4. Multiply the probability of each scenario by the benefit (or cost) in the scenario to get an *expected value.*

EXHIBIT 3-5 ■ Forecasting Benefits When it is Difficult to Predict the Future

① List Possible Scenarios	② Estimate Probability	③ Estimate Benefit	④ Calculate Expected Benefit
Recession	10%	× $50 =	$5
Moderate growth	70%	$100	$70
High growth	20%	$200	+ $40

⑤ $115

5. Add the expected values of each scenario to get the expected benefit (or cost).

Omit non-monetary costs and benefits. It is possible to put a monetary figure on intangible items. In fact, it is not uncommon for public policy studies to put a monetary value on human life. However, there are two reasonable arguments for only including monetary benefits and costs in the net present value calculation:

1. The analysis is simpler to perform—non-monetary benefits and costs such as human life and happiness are difficult and time consuming to quantify.
2. The overall analysis may be more accurate if non-monetary benefits and costs are left out of a net present value calculation.

How can this be? When a non-monetary cost or benefit is included in a net present value analysis, there is the tendency to consider these non-monetary factors twice. First, they are quantified in the net present value calculation. Then, after the net present value formula recommends a specific option as the best alternative, decision makers tend to distrust somewhat the recommendation, so they reconsider the importance of non-monetary factors, such as the human lives saved or the political ramifications. For this reason, it may be better to separate monetary and non-monetary considerations and have a clear picture of the monetary payoff and then compare it to the non-monetary considerations. Omitting non-monetary costs and benefits may also make an analysis more accurate because it would remove the danger of over or undervaluing non-monetary costs and benefits.

Step 2: Determine the Discount Rate

The discount rate converts the stream of future costs and benefits into their value today. For a private firm, the discount rate is simply the rate of return on an investment of comparable risk. Unfortunately, there is no consensus on how governments should determine their discount rate.

Economists agree that a government discount rate should measure two items:

1. A community's preference for present versus future consumption and
2. The opportunity cost of the funds used to finance a project.

Economists disagree, however, over *how* these items should be measured and what the government discount rate should be. Six methods of determining the government discount rate are discussed below. The first three methods view the opportunity cost of the funds as an opportunity cost to the *government*. Methods four and five view the opportunity cost as an opportunity cost to *citizens*. Method six uses ethical/political judgment to select a discount rate.

Method 1: Use the government's cost of borrowing. A commonly used method of selecting a discount rate is to use the local government's cost of long-term borrowing.[3] A government's cost of borrowing is approximately equal to the interest rate on its municipal bonds. Ideally, the maturity of the bond used to set the discount rate should be similar to the life of the project. One argument for using the cost of borrowing as the discount rate is that this rate represents a kind of minimum standard for the project to meet. If a project is financed with debt, its rate of return should be higher than the interest rate of the bond used to finance it. Otherwise, the government would be better off financially by not borrowing the money.

---

3. *Policy Analysis: Concepts and Practice*, by Aidan R. Vining and David L. Weimer, Englewood Cliffs, NJ: Prentice-Hall, Inc., 1992, p. 306. King County, Washington and the City of Portland, Oregon use the cost of long-term borrowing as the discount rate for long-term projects and the rate of return on their short-term investments as the discount rate for short-term projects. The General Accounting Office (GAO) also uses this method for the federal government. The GAO determines the discount rate by selecting the interest rate of Treasury bonds with the same maturity as the life of the project.

Method 2: Use the government's rate of return on short-term cash investments. Another commonly used method is to set the discount rate equal to the interest rate earned on the government's short-term cash portfolio. This interest rate reflects the government's opportunity cost for using funds for the proposed project. In other words, by selecting the proposed project, the government forgoes the interest that it could earn by keeping the funds in its investment portfolio.

Method 3: Use the discount rate at which the net benefit of displaced government projects is zero.[4] By selecting a proposed project, the government loses the opportunity of receiving the net benefits from alternative projects. Therefore, a proposed project should have a rate of return that is greater than alternative projects. This method sets the discount rate equal to the discount rate at which the net benefits of alternative projects are zero. This method is theoretically sound, but difficult to implement in practice because of the time required to do a return on investment analysis of all conceivable alternatives.

Method 4: For tax-financed projects, use the after-tax rate of return on Treasury bonds; for bond-financed projects, use the pre-tax rate of return on private investments.[5] This method views the opportunity cost of government projects as an opportunity cost to citizens.

If a project is tax-financed, then it displaces citizens' consumption in the current year, in exchange for consumption in some future year. The "exchange rate" that reflects society's preference for exchanging present for future consumption is reflected by the U.S. Treasury bond interest rates in the financial markets. One measure of this "exchange rate" is the after-tax rate of return on a U.S. Treasury bond with a maturity similar to the life of the project. By using this discount rate, a government's decisions to forgo current expenditures for future expenditures match society's preferences. For example, if society highly values forgoing current spending for spending in the future, then this preference will be reflected by a low interest rate. An argument can be made

---

4. *Government and Economic Choice: An Introduction to Public Finance*, by Thomas F. Pogue and L.G. Sgontz, Boston, MA: Houghton Mifflin Company, 1978, p. 156.
5. *A Guide to Benefit-Cost Analysis*, by Edward M. Gramlich, Englewood Cliffs, NJ: Prentice-Hall, Inc., 1990, pp. 109-110; *Government and Economic Choice: An Introduction to Public Finance*, by Thomas F. Pogue and L.G. Sgontz, Boston, MA: Houghton Mifflin Company, 1978, p. 156.

that government discount rates should also be low to reflect this preference.

If a project is bond-financed, then it displaces private investment dollars that may have gone to other investments. For a government project to be financially beneficial to society, its rate of return should be greater than this displaced private investment, otherwise society would be better off with the private investment. The discount rate in this instance should approximate the rate of return on the displaced private investment. One way of calculating this discount rate is to use the pre-tax rate of return on a long-term corporate or U.S. Treasury bond with a maturity and risk similar to the project.

Method 5: Use the rates of return on all sources of private capital that a project displaces weighted by the percent that is drawn from each source.[6] The previous method sets the discount rate equal to a specific interest rate depending on whether a project is financed through bonds or taxes. In actual practice, many projects are financed through *both* bonds and taxes and displace different types of private investment. This method attempts to more precisely determine the opportunity cost of displaced private investment by measuring the rate of return for each source of private capital and multiplying this by the percent drawn from that source. The sum of these weighted rates of return is the return that could have been realized by society if the funds were left in the private sector.

Method 6: None of the above — the choice of a discount rate is an ethical/political decision.[7] Some economists conclude that there is currently no analytical method for determining a government discount rate that is both practical and theoretically flawless.[8] As such, govern-

---

6. *Fiscal Administration: Analysis and Applications for the Public Sector*, by John L. Mikesell, Belmont, CA: Wadsworth Publishing Company, 1991, p. 188.
7. *Public Policy Analysis: An Introduction*, by William N. Dunn, Englewood Cliffs, NJ: Prentice-Hall, 1994, p. 266; *Basic Methods of Policy Analysis and Planning*, by Carl V. Patton and David S. Sawicki, Englewood Cliffs, NJ: Prentice-Hall, Inc., 1993, p. 283; *Government and Economic Choice: An Introduction to Public Finance*, by Thomas F. Pogue and L.G. Sgontz, Boston, MA: Houghton Mifflin Company, 1978, p. 158.
8. Economists have proposed additional methods for determining government discount rates including using multiple discount rates for different future time periods, different discount rates for discounting costs and benefits, and different discount rates for different types of projects. (Robert E. Goodin, "Discounting Discounting," *Journal of Public Policy*, volume 2, number I, pp. 53-72.)

EXHIBIT 3-6 ■ Preferred Method of Calculating a Government Discount Rate

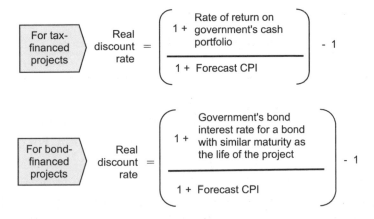

ments should use "reasoned judgment and ethical discourse" to determine their discount rate. However, the selection should remain within the confines of a standard range of discount rates and should be tested with sensitivity analysis (Tool 12).

Preferred Method: For tax-financed projects, use the real rate of return on the government's cash portfolio; for bond-financed projects, use the government's real bond interest rate; and test a range of discount rates with sensitivity analysis. Of the five methods of determining a discount rate, the author prefers to use a different discount rate for projects that are primarily financed with taxes and projects that are primarily financed with bonds.[9] I argue that tax-financed projects should have a discount rate that is different from bond-financed projects because the opportunity cost of capital is different for tax financing than for bond financing. In addition, tax financing displaces private consumption, whereas bond financing mostly displaces private investment.

Using this method (shown in Exhibit 3-6), projects that are financed primarily by taxes are given a discount rate equal to the real interest rate earned on the government's short-term cash portfolio. This interest rate reflects the opportunity cost of using government funds that might otherwise be invested. For projects that are financed by bonds, the discount rate is set equal to the real interest rate on the government's bonds of similar maturity. This interest rate reflects the government's cost of capital.

---

9. The Government Finance Officers Association does not have a recommended practice on setting a discount rate.

EXHIBIT 3-7 ■ Real to Nominal Conversion Formula

$$\left(1 + \frac{\text{Real}}{\text{discount rate}}\right) \times \left(1 + \frac{\text{Future}}{\text{CPI}}\right) - 1 = \frac{\text{Nominal}}{\text{discount rate}}$$

A significant advantage of this method is that it is straightforward and subject to minimal manipulation. Methods three, four, and five can be cumbersome and subject to an analyst's interpretation. For example, method five requires the calculation of the return on investment of all alternatives to a proposed project. This calculation is not only time-consuming, but also subject to an analyst's interpretation of what the possible alternatives are and what their return on investment is. In contrast, setting the discount rate equal to the government's investment return or bond interest rate is simple to determine and easy to obtain. In addition, it is relatively simple for decision makers to understand.

The following example shows how to calculate a real discount rate using the preferred method. Assuming a government earns an average rate of return of 5.1 percent and the forecast inflation rate is 2.6 percent, the real discount rate for tax-financed projects would be:

$$\left(\frac{1 + 0.051}{1 + 0.026}\right) - 1 = 0.024 = \boxed{2.4\%}$$

Assuming that the government's bond interest rate is 5.6 percent and the forecast inflation rate is 2.6 percent, the real discount rate for bond-financed projects would be:

$$\left(\frac{1 + 0.056}{1 + 0.026}\right) - 1 = 0.029 = \boxed{2.9\%}$$

It is important to remember that the formulas above calculate *real*, not nominal, discount rates. Thus, they should be used with forecasts of costs and benefits made in real (or current) dollars. If a real discount rate is used, care should be taken when comparing this rate to the rate used in other governments because other governments may be using a nominal discount rate. To compare a real discount rate to a nominal discount rate, use the formula in Exhibit 3-7 to convert a real discount rate to a nominal discount rate.

EXHIBIT 3-8 ▪ **Calculating the Net Present Value**

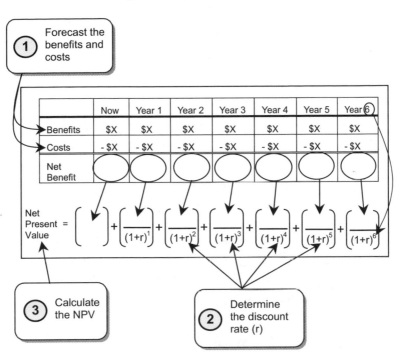

Step 3: Calculate the Net Present Value of Each Alternative

Use the diagram in Exhibit 3-8 to calculate a net present value for each alternative. First, combine the benefits and costs in each year to produce a net benefit for that year. Second, plug the net benefit of each year into the corresponding numerator in the formula below it. (Note that the exponent in each denominator corresponds to a particular year in the table above it.) Third, solve the formula to calculate the net present value for the alternative.[10]

Step 4: Determine Which Alternative Has the Highest Net Present Value

After calculating a net present value for each alternative, determine which alternative has the highest net present value. If only monetary costs and benefits were included in the calculation, then consider

---

10. Although Exhibit 3-8 only extends out to a six-year period, it could be extended to any length of time.

EXHIBIT 3-9 ■ Forecasted Costs and Benefits of Both Proposals

Proposal A									
		Year							
	Now	**1**	**2**	**3**	**4**	**5**	**6**	**7**	**8**
Benefits	$0	$0	$25k	$25k	$25k	$25k	$25k	$25k	$25k
Costs	−$1,000k	−$3,000k	−$40k	−$40k	−$40k	−$40k	−$40k	−$40k	−$40k
Net Benefit	−$1,000k	−$3,000k	−$15k	−$15k	−$15k	−$15k	−$15k	−$15k	−$15k

Proposal B									
		Year							
	Now	**1**	**2**	**3**	**4**	**5**	**6**	**7**	**8**
Benefits	$0	$0	$15k	$15k	$15k	$15k	$15k	$25k	$25k
Costs	−$1,000k	−$1,500k	−$20k	−$20k	−$20k	−$20k	−$1,700k	−$40k	−$40k
Net Benefit	−$1,000k	−$1,500k	−$5k	−$5k	−$5k	−$5k	−$1,685k	−$15k	−$15k

Opportunity   Construction   Maintenance
cost of land   costs   costs

whether the non-monetary costs and benefits justify selecting another alternative. For example, if a government determines that three capital projects (e.g., new bus, new train, and road widening) offer approximately the same net present value, then other non-monetary factors may tip the balance in favor of one proposal. Such factors might include improved service to the public or environmental benefits.

Example of a net present value analysis. To illustrate the first four steps, suppose a small city is considering building a set of public baseball diamonds on vacant land owned by the city. The Recreation Department presents two proposals. Proposal A is to build the entire park in the first year. Proposal B is to build half of the park in the first year and expand the park in the sixth year at a higher cost. Both proposals generate revenue from concession sales. Since the baseball diamonds would be located on city property, an opportunity cost of $1 million is included as the initial cost of both proposals. Exhibit 3-9 contains forecasts of the costs and benefits of both proposals.

EXHIBIT 3-10 ■ Calculating the Net Present Value of Both Proposals

$$\boxed{\text{Proposal A}}$$

$$\text{NPV} = \left(-\$1{,}000k\right) + \left(\frac{-\$3{,}000k}{(1+0.03)^1}\right) + \left(\frac{-\$15k}{(1+0.03)^2}\right) + \left(\frac{-\$15k}{(1+0.03)^3}\right) + \left(\frac{-\$15k}{(1+0.03)^4}\right) + \left(\frac{-\$15k}{(1+0.03)^5}\right) + \left(\frac{-\$15k}{(1+0.03)^6}\right) + \left(\frac{-\$15k}{(1+0.03)^7}\right) + \left(\frac{-\$15k}{(1+0.03)^8}\right)$$

$$-\$4{,}003k = \left(-\$1{,}000k\right) + \left(\frac{-\$3{,}000k}{(1.03)}\right) + \left(\frac{-\$15k}{(1.06)}\right) + \left(\frac{-\$15k}{(1.09)}\right) + \left(\frac{-\$15k}{(1.13)}\right) + \left(\frac{-\$15k}{(1.16)}\right) + \left(\frac{-\$15k}{(1.19)}\right) + \left(\frac{-\$15k}{(1.23)}\right) + \left(\frac{-\$15k}{(1.27)}\right)$$

$$\boxed{\text{Proposal B}}$$

$$\text{NPV} = \left(-\$1{,}000k\right) + \left(\frac{-\$1{,}500k}{(1+0.03)^1}\right) + \left(\frac{-\$5k}{(1+0.03)^2}\right) + \left(\frac{-\$5k}{(1+0.03)^3}\right) + \left(\frac{-\$5k}{(1+0.03)^4}\right) + \left(\frac{-\$5k}{(1+0.03)^5}\right) + \left(\frac{-\$1{,}685k}{(1+0.03)^6}\right) + \left(\frac{-\$5k}{(1+0.03)^7}\right) + \left(\frac{-\$5k}{(1+0.03)^8}\right)$$

$$-\$3{,}910k = \left(-\$1{,}000k\right) + \left(\frac{-\$1{,}500k}{(1.03)}\right) + \left(\frac{-\$5k}{(1.06)}\right) + \left(\frac{-\$5k}{(1.09)}\right) + \left(\frac{-\$5k}{(1.13)}\right) + \left(\frac{-\$5k}{(1.16)}\right) + \left(\frac{-\$1{,}685k}{(1.19)}\right) + \left(\frac{-\$5k}{(1.23)}\right) + \left(\frac{-\$5k}{(1.27)}\right)$$

Exhibit 3-10 shows the net present value calculation for both proposals. The example assumes a discount rate of 3 percent and that both options have a life of eight years. The analysis shows that Proposal B has the best net present value (i.e., lowest costs).

Step 5: Determine Whether the Best Alternative is Fundable

After determining which alternatives have the highest net present value, the next step is to evaluate whether the top alternatives are fundable. As someone might say, "Yeah, it's a good project, but can we afford it?" If this question cannot be answered with certainty or if a project is relatively large, a government should conduct a project affordability analysis to evaluate its ability to fund the proposed projects.

Project affordability analysis. A project affordability analysis identifies funding/financing options, determines the resources that are available with each option, and evaluates the options. The diagram in Exhibit 3-11 illustrates the steps in a project affordability analysis.

EXHIBIT 3-11 ■ Simplified Ilustration of a Project Affordability Analysis

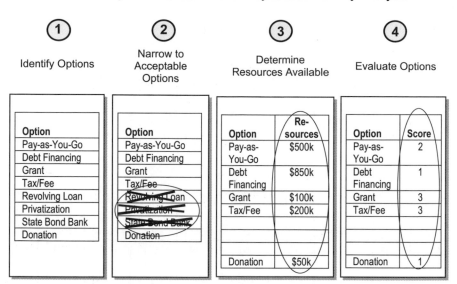

①	②	③	④
Identify Options	Narrow to Acceptable Options	Determine Resources Available	Evaluate Options

Option
Pay-as-You-Go
Debt Financing
Grant
Tax/Fee
Revolving Loan
Privatization
State Bond Bank
Donation

Option
Pay-as-You-Go
Debt Financing
Grant
Tax/Fee
Revolving Loan
Privatization
State Bond Bank
Donation

Option	Re-sources
Pay-as-You-Go	$500k
Debt Financing	$850k
Grant	$100k
Tax/Fee	$200k
Donation	$50k

Option	Score
Pay-as-You-Go	2
Debt Financing	1
Grant	3
Tax/Fee	3
Donation	1

1. Identify potential funding/financing options. The first step is simply to list all potential options for funding/financing the project. To assist the reader with this step, Exhibit 3-12 lists many of the financing options available to local governments.[11]

2. Narrow list to acceptable options. The second step is to eliminate all options that are illegal, politically unacceptable, or administratively infeasible. State statutes and local ordinances should be examined to determine whether options are legally available. For example, some states prohibit local governments from issuing certain types of debt instruments. In addition, certain options such as privatization and circumventing legal debt limitations may not be politically acceptable for some local governments. Finally, some options may not be administratively feasible. For example, most small governments would find it

---

11. The exhibit is intended only to show the universe of funding mechanisms, it is *not* intended to be an endorsement of any of these mechanisms. For a thorough discussion of these options see *Capital Improvement Programming: A Guide for Smaller Governments*, by Patricia Tigue, Chicago, IL: Government Finance Officers Association, 1996, chapter 8, "Evaluating Funding Options."

EXHIBIT 3-12 ■ Funding Mechanisms

1. Pay as You Go (PAYG)
   a. Operating budget revenues
   b. Capital improvement fund
   c. Fund balance reserves

2. Debt Financing
   a. General obligation bonds
   b. Revenue bonds
   c. Special assessment or special district bonds
   d. Tax increment financing bonds

3. Unconventional Debt Financing
   a. Floating rate bonds
   b. Zero coupon bonds
   c. Compound interest bonds
   d. Stripped coupon bonds
   e. Stepped interest bonds
   f. Put bonds
   g. Bonds with warrants

4. Short-term Borrowing
   a. Bond anticipation notes
   b. Grant anticipation notes
   c. Revenue anticipation notes
   d. Tax anticipation notes
   e. Tax-exempt commercial paper
   f. Tax-exempt demand master notes
   g. Capital notes

5. Leasing
   a. Lease-Purchase Agreements
   b. Certificates of Participation

6. Grants
   a. Federal grants
   b. State grants

7. Taxes/Fees
   a. User charges
   b. Impact fees/exactions
   c. Special taxes
   d. Special assessments

8. Revolving Loan Programs

9. State Bond Banks

10. Public/Private Partnerships

11. Private Contributions/Donations

---

infeasible to issue variable rate debt.[12]

3. Determine the resources that are available from each acceptable option. After narrowing the list of funding options, the next step is to determine the amount of funds that is available with each option.[13] An estimate should be made for every funding option for each year that resources are needed. Depending on the funding option, several techniques may be used to obtain this information. To determine available grant funds, a government would research federal and state govern-

---

12. This discussion is based on *Capital Improvement Programming: A Guide for Smaller Governments,* by Patricia Tigue, Chicago, IL: Government Finance Officers Association, 1996.
13. As it is very time consuming to determine the available resources for particular funding options, the author recommends that this analysis be limited to the most likely funding options.

EXHIBIT 3-13 ■ The Output of a Financial Capacity Analysis

General Fund Item (000s)	2002	2003	2004	2005	2006	2007
Projected operating revenue	$9,537	$10,103	$10,289	$10,475	$10,734	$10,982
Proceeds from bond issues	$400	$400	$1,000	$1,000	$700	$700
Fund balance/reserves	$220	$700	$810	$700	$730	$750
Total Resources	$10,157	$11,203	$12,099	$12,175	$12,164	$12,432
Projected operating expenditures	$8,230	$8,432	$8,752	$9,092	$9,310	$9,543
Debt service	$952	$984	$1,023	$993	$1,017	$1,093
Fund balance set aside as operating reserves or to meet unfunded liabilities (based on historical trend analysis)	$700	$810	$700	$730	$750	$770
Total Requirements	$9,882	$10,226	$10,475	$10,815	$11,077	$11,406
Net Capital Financing Potential	$275	$977	$1,624	$1,360	$1,087	$1,026

ment documents.[14] To determine funds available through debt financing, a government would conduct an analysis of debt capacity. (See Appendix B—Government Finance Officers Association Recommended Practice: Analysis of Debt Capacity.) To determine the amount of funds available through taxes and fees, a government may conduct a qualitative analysis of the political environment. Finally, to determine the amount of funds available through pay-as-you-go financing, a government would conduct a financial capacity analysis.[15] The steps involved in a financial capacity analysis are discussed below.

Financial Capacity Analysis. A financial capacity analysis begins by assessing a government's historical trends in revenues, expenditures, debt, operating position, and unfunded liabilities. This information is then used to forecast future revenues and expenditures for multiple

14. The federal government's *Catalog of Federal Domestic Assistance* is a comprehensive source of information on federal government grants and loans. On-line access to this document is available at http://www.cfda.gov/. Another source of information on federal assistance to local governments is the U.S. State and Local Gateway at http://www.statelocal.gov/funding.html. A list of state governments' single points of contact is available at http://www.cfda.gov/public/cat-spocs.asp. The Foundation Center provides information on private-sector funding. The web address is http://fdncenter.org/.

15. This discussion of financial capacity analysis is based on *Capital Improvement Programming: A Guide for Smaller Governments*, by Patricia Tigue, Chicago, IL: Government Finance Officers Association, 1996, chapter 7, "Evaluating the Ability to Fund Capital Projects." The reader should consult this publication for a more complete discussion of this technique.

years. Multiple forecasts are generated using pessimistic, moderate, and optimistic assumptions. In the final step, the revenue and expenditure forecasts are used to estimate the amount that is available in the budget for capital projects. Exhibit 3-13 shows an example of the output of the final step of a financial capacity analysis.

4. Evaluate funding options. The final step in a project affordability analysis is to evaluate funding options based on their equity, effectiveness, and efficiency. *Equity* refers to the extent to which those who benefit from a project are the ones who pay for it. For example, it can be argued that a project with a useful life of 30 years should be financed with debt (paid back over time) rather than current reserves because it will benefit residents in the future. *Effectiveness* refers to the ability of a funding option to provide a sufficient amount of funds when it is needed. For example, a state grant may not supply funds on the date that they are needed by the local government. *Efficiency* refers to the administrative and monetary cost of a funding option. For example, debt financing entails interest costs and issuance costs, as well as staff time to administer the debt. A net present value calculation can be used to compare the costs of funding options.

A convenient method to compare the equity, effectiveness, and efficiency of funding options is a weighted score table (see decision tool 3). In Exhibit 3-14, a weighted score table is used to compare pay-as-you-go financing, debt financing, and a state grant. First, the three guiding principles of equity, effectiveness, and efficiency were weighted. Second, a score of one to ten was given to each funding option for each criteria. Finally, the scores were multiplied by the weights to calculate weighted scores, which were summed to calculate a total weighted score.

Limitations of Tool

The main limitation of net present value analysis is the difficulty of accurately forecasting future costs and benefits. For example, programs can have unanticipated costs or generate less revenue than expected. Another limitation of net present value analysis is that there is no universal discount rate or standard method of setting a discount rate. Because there is no standard in this area, net present value analysis is vulnerable to manipulation through selecting a high or low discount rate.

EXHIBIT 3-14 ▪ Using a Weighted Score Table to Compare Funding Options

Criteria	Weights	Pay-as-You-Go		Debt Financing		State Grant	
		Score	Weighted score	Score	Weighted score	Score	Weighted score
Equity	.60	5	3.0	8	4.8	5	3.0
Effectiveness	.80	6	4.8	4	3.2	2	1.6
Efficiency	.30	5	1.5	2	0.6	8	2.4
Total Weighted Score			9.3		8.6		7.0

Both of these weaknesses may be addressed by conducting a sensitivity analysis.

TOOL 8: RETURN ON INVESTMENT ANALYSIS

Return on investment analysis[16] (ROI) evaluates a project's costs and benefits over time to determine the likelihood that a project will break even. Like net present value analysis, ROI forecasts the costs and benefits of a project in each future year and discounts these costs and benefits to a present value. However, instead of selecting a single discount rate, ROI recalculates the net present value many times using a large range of discount rates. The many recalculations determine how low the discount rate would have to be for the net present value to equal zero (i.e., for the project to break even).

As discussed earlier, the *discount rate* is like an exchange rate that converts dollars in the future to dollars today. When a project has future costs and benefits, a discount rate is used to convert the future value of these costs and benefits into their present value. The discount rate usually reflects a government's cost of borrowing or a community's preference for present versus future consumption. For example, a community will have a low discount rate when it has a low cost of borrowing or a strong preference for investing in the future. An ROI analysis does not calculate the government's discount rate, but calculates a kind of mini-

---

16. Return on investment analysis is also known as "internal rate of return analysis" and "discounted cash-flow rate of return analysis."

EXHIBIT 3-15 ■ **The Output of a Return on Investment Analysis**

Discount Rate	Net Present Value
0%	$450
1%	$420
2%	$390
3%	$360
4%	$330
5%	$300
6%	$270
7%	$240
8%	$210
9%	$180
10%	$150
11%	$120
12%	$90
13%	$60
14%	$30
15%	$0

Net Present Value

Net present value of project at various discount rates

$500k

$250k

$500k

5%   10%   15%   20%   25%   Discount Rate

−$250k

−$500k

Range of likely discount rates

mum standard that the government's discount rate would have to meet in order for a project to break even. For example, if an ROI analysis shows that a project breaks even at a discount rate of 30 percent, then the project would generate a positive rate of return if the government had a discount rate below 30 percent. Since a government's real discount rate is likely to be around 0.5 percent to 5 percent, then this project would not only break even, but also generate a high return on the investment.

The table and chart in Exhibit 3-15 show the type of output that an ROI analysis generates. In the chart, the horizontal axis shows a range of possible government discount rates. The vertical axis shows a range of possible net present values for the project. The downward sloping line shows the project's net present value at different discount rates. This line is the result of recalculating the net present value many times using different discount rates. A shaded bar shows the likely range of the government's discount rate. Note that the project has a positive net present value for discount rates even far above this range, thus it is very likely to break even. The point at which the sloping line crosses the x-axis is the discount rate at which the project breaks even. This point is also the project's rate of return.

Step 1: Forecast the Benefits and Costs in Each Year

Forecast the total benefits and total costs in each year. Make all forecasts in today's dollars (i.e., real dollars). It is important to treat inflation consistently throughout the calculation, so all forecasts should be made in *real* dollars, and discounted at a *real* discount rate.[17]

		Year					
	Now	1	2	3	4	5	6
Benefits	$0	$52	$47	$47	$47	$47	$47
Costs	–$950	–$40	–$40	–$40	–$40	–$40	–$40

If the benefits and costs are difficult to forecast, calculate an *expected value* (Tool 2) for each benefit and cost.

Step 2: Calculate the Net Present Value Using a Range of Discount Rates

Use the diagram in Exhibit 3-16 to calculate the project's net present value at a particular discount rate. First, combine the benefits and costs in each year to produce a net benefit for that year. Second, plug the net benefit of each year into the corresponding numerator in the formula below it. (Note that the exponent in each denominator corresponds to a particular year in the table above it.) Third, solve the formula to calculate the net present value at a particular discount rate. Fourth, recalculate the formula using a different discount rate for each recalculation. Recalculate the net present value for a broad range of discount rates (e.g., 0 percent to 50 percent).[18]

---

17. It is also possible to make all forecasts in nominal dollars and discount them at a nominal discount rate. In either case, inflation should be treated consistently.
18. Although the Exhibit 3-16 only extends out to a six-year period, it could be extended to any length of time.

EXHIBIT 3-16 ■ **Calculating a Return on Investment Analysis**

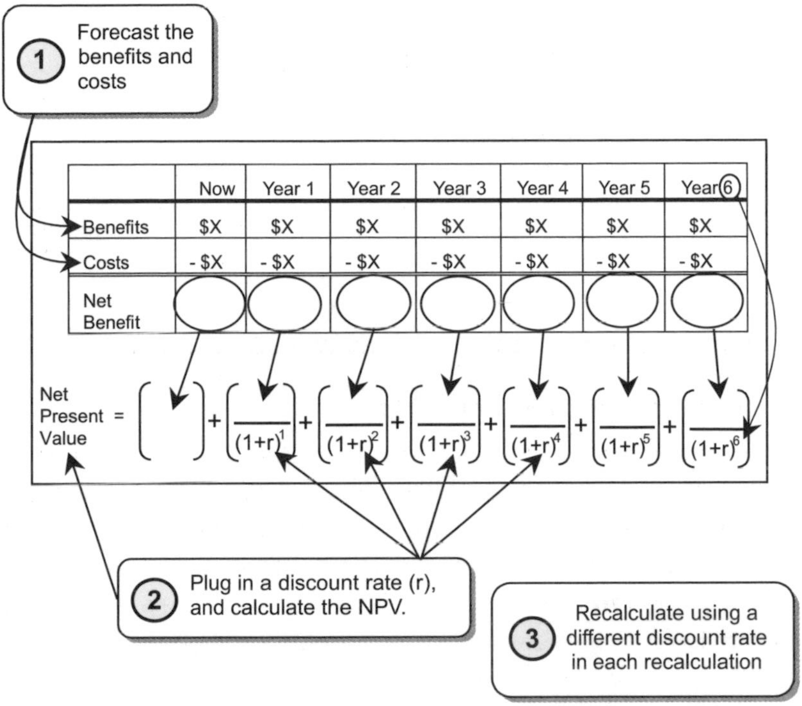

① Forecast the benefits and costs

	Now	Year 1	Year 2	Year 3	Year 4	Year 5	Year ⑥
Benefits	$X	$X	$X	$X	$X	$X	$X
Costs	- $X	- $X	- $X	- $X	- $X	- $X	- $X
Net Benefit							

$$\text{Net Present Value} = \left(\downarrow\right) + \frac{\downarrow}{(1+r)^1} + \frac{\downarrow}{(1+r)^2} + \frac{\downarrow}{(1+r)^3} + \frac{\downarrow}{(1+r)^4} + \frac{\downarrow}{(1+r)^5} + \frac{\downarrow}{(1+r)^6}$$

② Plug in a discount rate (r), and calculate the NPV.

③ Recalculate using a different discount rate in each recalculation

Step 3: Graph the Project's Net Present Value at Different Discount Rates

Plot a graph similar to the example in Exhibit 3-17 by using the results of step 2.

Step 4: Determine Whether the Project is Likely to Break Even

Finally, using the graph from the previous step, compare the discount rate at which the project's net present value is zero to the likely range of the government's discount rate. If the project has a zero net present value at a discount rate that is higher than the government's discount rate, then the project is likely to break even.

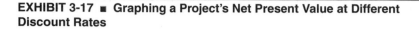

EXHIBIT 3-17 ▪ Graphing a Project's Net Present Value at Different Discount Rates

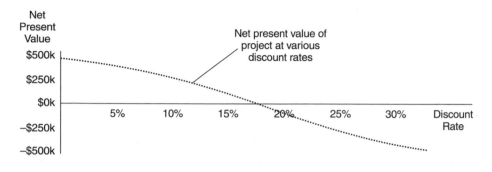

Caveats When Using ROI Analysis

ROI analysis should not be used when a project's net benefits in future years alternate from positive to negative. Many projects have a negative net benefit in the first year, when the initial investment is made, and then positive net benefits in subsequent years. However, another possibility is that a project has some future years that generate a net benefit, and other future years that generate a net cost. ROI should not be used for these cases because it calculates a zero net present value at multiple discount rates. In cases when a project's net benefits in future years alternate from positive to negative, the net present value tool should be used.

ROI analysis is also not well suited for deciding between alternatives. It is possible for an alternative to breakeven at a higher discount rate (i.e., have a higher rate of return), but be an inferior project because it has a lower net present value at the government's discount rate. The chart in Exhibit 3-18 illustrates this. The chart shows the net present values of two projects at various discount rates. Note that project A has a higher rate of return, but has a lower net present value than project B at the government's discount rate.

Net present value analysis is a better tool than ROI for deciding between alternatives. However, ROI can still be useful. If the discount rate is highly uncertain, ROI analysis could be used as a type of sensitivity analysis to see if a project is worthwhile over a broad range of discount rates. For example, the graph in Exhibit 3-18 shows that project B is better than project A only when the discount rate is lower than 10 percent.

EXHIBIT 3-18 ■ ROI Analysis May Incorrectly Identify the Best Alternative

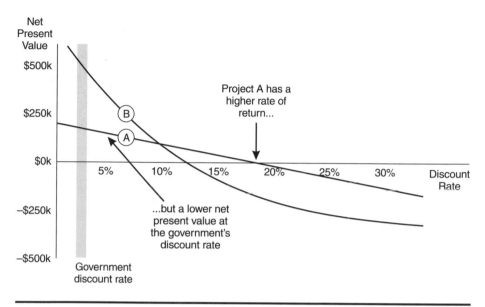

TOOL 9: COST-BENEFIT ANALYSIS

A cost-benefit analysis determines whether a project's benefits are greater than its costs. As a first step, all of a project's benefits are summed to calculate a project's total benefit, then all of the costs are summed to calculate a project's total cost. The total cost is then subtracted from the total benefit to calculate the project's total net benefit. If the total net benefit is a positive number, then the benefits are greater than the costs.

Because the scope of a cost-benefit analysis is much larger than the jurisdiction of a local government, it may not be a suitable analysis tool for many decisions. Cost-benefit analyses are sometimes conducted in many different ways; however, a *proper* cost-benefit analysis includes not only the costs and benefits to a local government, but all of the costs and benefits to the *entire society*. This means that a city that is considering building a refuse incinerator should calculate the costs and benefits of the incinerator to residents inside *and* outside the city.

Although calculating the costs and benefits to non-local residents is beneficial to society as a whole, it is not useful for local government officials who are only responsible for those residents within their jurisdiction. There are two variations of cost-benefit analysis, however, that are

EXHIBIT 3-19 ▪ A Cost-Benefit Analysis

Benefits		Costs	
Time savings	$15,000,000	Construction	$22,000,000
Safety benefits	$8,000,000	Maintenance	$800,000
Fee revenue	$1,600,000	User fees	$1,600,000
Operating cost savings	$2,300,000		
Total Benefit	$26,900,000	Total Cost	$24,400,000

Total Benefit	$26,900,000
— Total Cost	$24,400,000
Total Net Benefit	**$2,500,000**

more useful to local government officials. One variation is to separate the costs and benefits into local and non-local components. This variation shows the impact of a project on a government's residents. Another variation is fiscal impact analysis, which only measures the impact of a project on a particular local government's budget. Tool 10 discusses fiscal impact analysis.

Step 1: Identify All Costs and Benefits

There are five main steps to a cost-benefit analysis. The first step is to identify all of the benefits and costs to the entire society. Since local governments are usually most interested in the costs and benefits to their own residents, local governments will find a cost-benefit analysis most useful by separating costs and benefits into three categories: the local government, residents and businesses in the jurisdiction, and non-residents outside the jurisdiction. This breakdown can also help to prevent errors in an analysis, such as counting increased tax revenue in the total benefit of a project when it is actually just a transfer from residents to the government. With this breakdown, increased tax revenue would be counted as a benefit in the local government category, and a cost in the resident category. It would thus be cancelled out[19] as a net benefit.

---

19. The increased tax revenue may generate a net cost to society because the increased revenue may also entail a greater administrative cost to the government.

EXHIBIT 3-20 ■ Steps to a Cost-Benefit Analysis

1. Identify all costs and benefits.
2. Convert all costs and benefits into a monetary value.
3. Discount future costs and benefits to their present value.
4. Sum the costs and benefits to calculate the total cost and total benefit.

For each of the three categories of costs, list all of the costs and benefits that the project will generate. Include monetary costs and benefits (such as equipment costs, wages, tax revenue generated) and non monetary costs (such as hours saved, lives saved, and amount of environmental degradation).

A cost-benefit analysis can be rendered useless if it does not correctly identify costs and benefits. For this reason, it is useful to define several rules for what constitutes a cost or a benefit.

Rule 1: Consider All Benefits and Costs Relative to the Status Quo

If a proposal replaces an existing program, facility, equipment, or state of affairs, then count the benefits and costs if the replacement is made. For example, let's say that a county government is considering building a bridge across a river to replace a ferry that the county operates. A cost-benefit analysis might include operation and maintenance costs as a cost of the bridge. Let's say that the operation and maintenance costs are $100,000 per year. An analyst might then include $100,000 of operation and maintenance costs in the "cost" column of a cost-benefit analysis. Although this seems reasonable, a serious mistake has just been made in the analysis: the analyst did not *compare this cost with the status quo* of a ferry. The operation and maintenance cost of the ferry is $400,000 per year. So the bridge would actually save the county $300,000 annually in operation and maintenance costs. Therefore, the operation and maintenance of the bridge is not a cost of $100,000 per year, but a *benefit* of $300,000 per year (see Exhibit 3-21).

To understand this rule, it is important to realize that a proposal's costs and benefits are really *relative* costs and benefits, not *actual* costs and benefits. In the example just given, the proposal's actual costs for operations and maintenance were $100,000. However, its *relative* costs are -$300,000. (A negative cost is a savings.) Exhibit 3-22 shows the formulas for calculating a proposal's relative cost and benefit.

EXHIBIT 3-21 ■ An Example of Calculating Costs Relative to the Status Quo

Status Quo (Ferry):

Benefits		Costs	
Time savings	$	Construction	$
Safety benefits	$	Operation & Maintenance	$400
Fee revenue	$	User fees	$
Total Benefit	$	Total Cost	$

Proposal (Bridge):

Benefits		Costs		
Time savings	$	Construction		$
Safety benefits	$	Operation & Maintenance	Proposal's actual cost	$100
			Status quo cost	- $400
			Proposal's relative cost	-$300
Fee revenue	$	User fees		$
Total Benefit	$		Total Cost	$

Another mistake is to not include costs that would be avoided if the proposal is selected. For example, a ferry might have insurance costs that will be avoided by operating a bridge. These insurance costs should be included as a benefit of the bridge, and noted as "insurance costs avoided."

Rule 2: Consider Whether a Benefit to One Party is a Cost to Another Party, and Vice Versa

In the bridge example, the county government would lose the revenue generated by the ferry service. This would be recorded as a cost (or loss) to the government. However, the ferry revenue lost should also be counted as a benefit to river crossers, and should be recorded as a benefit to residents and non-residents. The same is true for bridge construction costs. This is included in the cost column for the government and in the benefit column as "employment income for residents and non-residents."

Rule 3: Do Not Double Count Costs and Benefits

A cost-benefit analysis should not count an item as both a cost of one proposal and the benefit of another. An example of this would be to

---

EXHIBIT 3-22 ■ Calculating Relative Costs and Benefits

$$\left(\begin{array}{c} \text{Proposal's} \\ \text{relative cost} \end{array}\right) = \left(\begin{array}{c} \text{Proposal's} \\ \text{actual cost} \end{array}\right) - \left(\begin{array}{c} \text{Status quo} \\ \text{cost} \end{array}\right)$$

$$\left(\begin{array}{c} \text{Proposal's} \\ \text{relative benefit} \end{array}\right) = \left(\begin{array}{c} \text{Proposal's} \\ \text{actual benefit} \end{array}\right) - \left(\begin{array}{c} \text{Status quo} \\ \text{benefit} \end{array}\right)$$

---

count "insurance costs" as a cost of the ferry service *and* "insurance costs avoided" as a benefit of the bridge.

Step 2: Convert All Costs and Benefits to a Monetary Value

Once all of the costs and benefits have been specified, the second step is to convert all of the costs and benefits into a monetary value. Converting all of the costs and benefits into a monetary value permits us to add together all of the individual costs and benefits to calculate a total cost and total benefit, which can then be used to calculate a total net benefit. Without converting to a monetary value, the cost-benefit analysis remains a list of individual costs and benefits in different units; some may be in dollars, but other costs and benefits may be in hours saved, amount of environmental degradation, lives saved, and satisfaction generated.

Needless to say, placing a dollar value on intangible items such as human life and happiness is controversial; however, it is a sensible alternative and is common in public policy analysis. In actuality, every human life is invaluable; however, *governments* implicitly place a finite value on human life in many decisions. If governments did not implicitly place a value on human life, then every project that could save one human life would be justified regardless of the costs because the benefits would be infinite. Since governments have finite resources, they must place a finite value on human life. It is better that this valuation be explicit rather than implicit.

There are five main methods[20] of valuing intangible items such as human life, time saved, and satisfaction with a public park. The following paragraphs will explain each of these methods. To assist the reader to value intangible items, Exhibit 3-23 presents common values for many intangible benefits and costs.

---

20. This discussion of valuing benefits and costs is based on *Public Policy Analysis: An Introduction*, by William N. Dunn, Englewood Cliffs, NJ: Prentice-Hall, Inc., 1994, pp. 320-321.

Method 1: Prices of Comparable Items

In this method, an analyst searches for goods and services in the marketplace that are comparable to the intangible item being valued. For example, to place a dollar value on the satisfaction generated by a public gym, an analyst would use the membership fee at a comparable private gym. To place a dollar value on 15 minutes that are saved by a new bridge, an analyst might use the value given to 15 minutes of work at the average hourly wage.

Method 2: Analyze Consumers' Willingness to Pay for an Intangible Item

In this method, an analyst places a monetary value on intangible items by observing the prices that consumers are willing to pay for the intangible item. For example, to place a monetary value on time, an analyst could look at the prices that consumers are willing to pay for an airline ticket to save five hours of travel time. If a six-hour bus trip costs $25 and a one-hour flight to the same city costs $100, then consumers are willing to pay $75 to save five hours. In other words, the value of saving one hour of travel time is $15.

An analyst might place a monetary value on human life by analyzing consumer's willingness to pay for safety items that will reduce the risk of death. For example, if consumers are willing to pay $200 for an airbag that will reduce the risk of death in a head-on collision by 70 percent, then this reduction of the risk of death is worth $200.

Method 3: Analyze Consumers' Willingness to Pay Indirect Costs to Obtain an Intangible Benefit

For example, to place a monetary value on the satisfaction generated by a state park, an analyst could calculate the expense that visitors are willing to incur to travel to the park. This travel cost is the monetary value that visitors give to the park.

Method 4: Survey Residents to Ask Them What They are Willing to Pay

In this method, an analyst simply asks residents what they are willing to pay to obtain certain intangible benefits. This method assumes that survey respondents will provide honest answers.

Method 5: Calculate the Replacement Cost or the Cost to Reverse a Negative Impact

In this method, an analyst puts a dollar value on an intangible item like environmental degradation by determining the cost of cleaning up the environmental degradation through reforestation, water purification, etc. In another example, the cost of losing a public park would be the cost of replacing the park by purchasing land and constructing a park at another site. This method assumes that the cost of restoring the status quo reflects its value. This might not be the case. For example, an existing park might be given a high value because it is expensive to replace, but actually have a low value because residents dislike it.

Common Values of Some Intangible Benefits and Costs

The values given to intangible costs and benefits can be the most controversial part of a cost-benefit analysis. Proponents of a project can make a project seem worthwhile by inflating the value of its intangible benefits. Likewise, opponents can inflate the values of its costs. Fortunately, public policy research has produced somewhat of a standard value, or standard range of values, for some intangible benefits and costs. Exhibit 3-23 lists the common values of several intangible benefits and costs and the source for each value.

Step 3: Discount Future Costs

The third basic step in a cost-benefit analysis is to discount the future costs and benefits of the project to their present value. (For a discussion of this step, see "Tool 7: Net Present Value Analysis.")

Step 4: Sum Costs and Benefits

The fourth step is to sum the monetary values given to all of the costs and benefits to calculate the total cost and total benefit of the project.

Step 5: Calculate the Total Net Benefit

The fifth step is to calculate the total net benefit by subtracting the total cost from the total benefit. The total net benefit is the bottom line of the cost-benefit analysis—it indicates whether the project is worthwhile. In general, a positive total net benefit indicates a worthwhile project because the benefits are greater than the costs. However, in some in-

EXHIBIT 3-23 ■ Values Given to Intangible Items in Public Policy Literature

Intangible Cost or Benefit	Specific Measure	Cost Per person (2001 US$)	Source	Description
Life		$1.6 to $5.1 mil. Average: $3.2 mil.	Ted R. Miller, *Narrowing the Plausible Range Around the Value of Life*, Washington, DC: The Urban Institute, 1989	Reviewed 49 studies that estimated the value of life. Selected 29 high quality studies and summarized estimates. Studies use 4 methods for valuing life.
		$2.6 to $13.7 mil.	Ann Fisher, Lauraine Chestnut, Daniel Violette, "The Value of Reducing Risks of Death: A Note on New Evidence," *Journal of Policy Analysis and Management*, vol. 8, no. 1, Winter 1989, p. 88-100.	Reviewed 21 studies that estimated the value of life. Studies use 3 methods for valuing life.
		$0.09 to $20.2 mil.	W. Kip Viscusi, "The Value of Risks to Life and Health," *Journal of Economic Literature*, vol. 31, no. 4, December 1993, p. 1912-1946.	Reviewed 37 studies that estimated the value of life. Studies use 3 methods for valuing life.
	Most Reasonable Estimate	**$2.7 to $4.1 million**	Conservative estimate based on the three reviews above.	

Source: Boardman, Greenberg, Vining, Weimer, *Cost-Benefit Analysis: Concepts and Practice* (Upper Saddle River, New Jersey: Prentice-Hall, 1996), pp. 377-391.

EXHIBIT 3-23 (continued) ■ **Values Given to Intangible Items in Public Policy Literature**

Intangible Cost or Benefit	Specific Measure	Cost Per person (2001 US$)	Source	Description
Injuries	Motor vehicle injuries	$14,848	Dorthy P. Rice, Ellen J. MacKenzie, and Associates, *Cost of Injury in the United States: A Report to Congress*, San Francisco, CA: Institute for Health and Aging, University of California and Injury Prevention Center, The Johns Hopkins University, 1989.	Major report for Congress. Very conservative estimates. Estimates include medical and rehabilitation costs and forgone earnings, but do not include pain and suffering, or property damage, court costs or other costs related to the injury.
	Falls	$4,969		
	Firearm injuries	$88,201		
	Poisonings	$8,217		
	Fire injuries and burns	$4,291		
	Drownings and near drownings	$106,489		
	Other injuries	$1,945		
	Injuries resulting in a future fatality	$519,707		
	Injuries requiring hospitalization	$55,898		
	Injuries not requiring hospitalization	$849		
	Work-related injuries	$33,722 to $67,445	W. Kip Viscusi, "The Value of Risks to Life and Health," *Journal of Economic Literature*, vol. 31, no. 4, December 1993, p. 1912-1946.	Reviewed 14 labor market studies conducted between 1978 and 1991.
Motor Vehicle Crashes	Average cost of non-fatal crashes	$59,470	Ted R. Miller, "Costs and Functional Consequences of Roadway Crashes," *Accident Analysis and Prevention*, vol. 25, no. 5, 1993, p. 593-607.	Estimates the comprehensive costs of U.S. motor vehicle crashes. Costs include: medical and emergency services, lost wages and household production, workplace disruption, insurance administration costs, legal proceedings, lost quality of life.
	Average cost of fatal crashes	$3,554,449		
	Injuries to spinal cord	$2,174,380		
	Injuries to lower extremity	$212,111		
	Injuries to brain	$126,066		
	Injuries to upper extremity	$82,465		
	Injuries to trunk/abdomen	$62,777		
	Injuries to face, other head, other neck	$24,274		
	Minor external injuries	$5,887		

EXHIBIT 3-23 (continued) ■ **Values Given to Intangible Items in Public Policy Literature**

Intangible Cost or Benefit	Specific Measure	Cost Per person (2001 US$)	Source	Description
Crime	Robbery (cost per victim)	$35,469	Ted R. Miller, Mark A. Cohen, and Shelli Rossman, "Victim Costs of Violent Crime and Resulting Injuries," *Health Affairs*, vol. 12, no. 4, 1993, p. 186-197.	Estimate the total costs of violent crimes. Costs include: direct costs (medical care, mental health and emergency response services, insurance administration), opportunity costs (forgone wages, fringe benefits, and housework), and costs of pain and suffering. Does not include costs of lost property.
	Assault (cost per victim)	$31,725		
	Arson (cost per victim)	$70,524		
	Murder (cost per victim)	$3,393,852		
	All firearm injuries	$72,612	Wendy Max and Dorothy P. Rice, "Shooting in the Dark; Estimating the Costs of Firearm Injuries," *Health Affairs*, vol. 12, no. 4, 1993, p. 171-185.	Estimate the costs of firearm injuries resulting from crimes and accidents. Costs include: direct costs (medical and hospital, rehabilitation, medication, and transportation costs) indirect costs (value of household labor, morbidity, and mortality costs)
	Fatal firearm injuries	$503,838		
	Firearm injuries requiring hospitalization	$44,729		
	Firearm injuries that do not require hospitalization	$618		
	Murder (Cost per arrested criminal)	$72,053	David A. Long, Charles D. Mallar, and Craig V. Thornton, "Evaluating the Benefits and Costs of the Jobs Corps," *Journal of Policy Analysis and Management*, 1, no. 1, Fall 1981, p. 55-76.	Estimates of costs include: criminal justice system costs, costs of personal injury and property damage, and losses associated with stolen property. May underestimate the cost of property loss because part of the loss is counted as a benefit to thieves.
	Assault(Cost per arrested criminal)	$7,948		
	Robbery (Cost per arrested criminal)	$35,164		
	Burglary (Cost per arrested criminal)	$17,141		
	Larceny and motor vehicle theft (Cost per arrested criminal)	$7,616		
	Drug law violations (Cost per arrested criminal)	$7,616		
	Other personal crimes (Cost per arrested criminal)	$2,199		
	Other miscellaneous crimes (Cost per arrested criminal)	$2,674		

EXHIBIT 3-23 (continued) ■ **Values Given to Intangible Items in Public Policy Literature**

Intangible Cost or Benefit	Specific Measure	Cost Per person (2001 US$)	Source	Description
Time	Value of travel time saved (intraurban/commuting travel)	40% to 50% of average hourly wage	W.G. Waters II, "Variations in the Value of Travel Time Savings: Empirical Studies and the Values for Road Project Evaluation," Working Paper, Faculty of Commerce, University of British Columbia, October 1993.	Reviewed 56 empirical studies conducted between 1974 and 1990.
Recreation	Picnicking	$13 to $53	Cindy F. Sorg and John B. Loomis, *Empirical Estimates of Amenity Forest Values: A Comparative Review*, General Technical Report RM-107, Fort Collins, CO: Rocky Mountain Forest and Range Experiment Station, Forest Service, USDA, 1984.	Combines the findings of numerous studies into a common value: benefit per day spent in recreational activity.
	Wilderness recreation	$24 to $135		
	Hiking	$15 to $84		
	Camping	$11 to $48		
	Downhill skiing	$44		
	Water sports	$18 to $49		
	Boating	$11 to $79		
	Cold water fishing	$16 to $124		
	Warm water fishing	$27 to $48		
	Salmon and steelhead sport fishing	$48 to $181		
	Big game hunting	$33 to $241		
	Small game hunting	$29 to $79		

stances, a government is not interested in the net benefit to the entire society, but the net benefit to *its residents* or *the local government*.

Limitations of Tool

An important limitation of cost-benefit analysis is the difficulty of converting intangible costs and benefits into a monetary value. It is very difficult to place a dollar value on benefits such as public safety and resident happiness. In addition, once a valuation has been made it may not be trusted.

Another limitation of cost-benefit analysis is that it is too time consuming to use for most decisions. Most of the other tools in this book simplify decisions by focusing an analysis on a few key factors. In contrast, cost-benefit analysis attempts to provide a *complete* analysis by taking into account all monetary and non-monetary costs and benefits to the entire society. This makes cost-benefit analysis a "heavy duty" decision tool.

TOOL 10: FISCAL IMPACT ANALYSIS

Fiscal impact analysis is basically a cost-benefit analysis that only considers the financial costs and benefits to a particular government, rather than the costs and benefits to the entire society. A fiscal impact study is usually conducted to predict the budgetary impact of a large-scale project such as a new land development, major annexation, or tax incentive program that will have a long-term effect. In general, a fiscal impact analysis will forecast a local government's revenues and expenditures over a five- to ten-year period with and without a proposed project.

There are many methods of conducting a fiscal impact analysis. Methods differ in accuracy and analytical complexity. This publication discusses the following four methods of fiscal impact analysis.[21]

- Simplified per capita cost method;
- Per capita multiplier method;
- Case study method; and,
- Service standard method.

---

21. Most of the discussion in this section is based on *The Fiscal Impact Guidebook: Estimating Local Costs and Revenues of Land Development*, Department of Housing and Urban Development, Washington, DC: U.S. Government Printing Office, 1979.

EXHIBIT 3-24 ■ Simplified Per Capita Cost Method

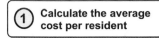

(1) **Calculate the average cost per resident**

$$\frac{\text{Current total local government expenditures}}{\text{Current population}} = \$ \text{ Cost / Resident}$$

Example:

$$\frac{\$55,000,000 \text{ total expenditures}}{40,000 \text{ residents}} = \$ 1,375 / \text{resident}$$

(2) **Multiply the Cost Per Resident by the Number of New Residents**

(\$Cost / resident) x (Number of new residents) = Additional cost of proposal

Example:

(\$1,375 / resident) x (5,000 new residents) = \$6,875,000

Several other important fiscal impact methods not covered in this publication include: econometric techniques (such as the proportional valuation method and the employment anticipation method), micro-simulation, and the comparable cities method.

Simplified Per Capita Cost Method

The simplified per capita cost method is a useful tool to obtain a rough estimate of the fiscal impact of a proposed residential development. To use this technique, an analyst calculates the average expenditures per resident, and then multiplies the cost per resident by the expected number of new residents due to a proposed residential development.

To illustrate how to use this method, suppose a village government is considering annexing an area with 5,000 residents. The first step is to divide the current total village expenditure[22] by the current population to calculate the average expenditure per resident (see Exhibit 3-24).

---

22. Total expenditures should include general fund expenditures (e.g., police, fire, parks, and roads) and all other expenditures for which the local government is responsible (e.g., water and sewer utility expenditures).

Suppose the current total expenditure is $55 million and the village has 40,000 residents; the cost per resident, then, would be $1,375.

The second step is to multiply the cost per resident by the expected number of new residents due to the proposed residential development. Since the cost per resident is $1,375 and there are 5,000 new residents, then the annexation will cost roughly $6.9 million in additional village expenditures.

It should be noted that the simplified per capita cost technique provides only a rough estimation of local government costs. This technique will tend to overestimate the cost per resident because it uses *total* local expenditures to calculate the cost per resident. *Total local government expenditures* includes some expenditures that are not directly attributable to the number of residents, such as expenditures to service commercial and industrial property. A more accurate estimation of the cost per resident would separate out the residential portion of total expenditures and divide it by the number of residents. The next method, per capita multiplier, makes this adjustment.

Per Capita Multiplier Method

The per capita multiplier method is designed to predict the fiscal impact of a residential development such as a new apartment complex or subdivision of single family homes. This method estimates fiscal impact by multiplying a government's current residential-related per capita expenditures by the expected number of new residents. The method uses a particular procedure for estimating both of these figures.

To determine a government's current residential-related per capita expenditures, this method separates out the residential-related portion of total expenditures[23] based on the proportion of the community's total property value that is residential (see Exhibit 3-25). The residential-related expenditures are then divided by the current population to calculate the expenditures per capita.

To determine the number of new residents, this method multiplies the number of new housing units by the average number of residents for that type of housing unit. The average number of residents for various types of housing units is available from Census data. The individ-

---

23. Total expenditures should include general fund expenditures (e.g., police, fire, parks, and roads) and all other expenditures for which the local government is responsible (e.g., water and sewer utility expenditures).

EXHIBIT 3-25 ■ Per Capita Multiplier Method

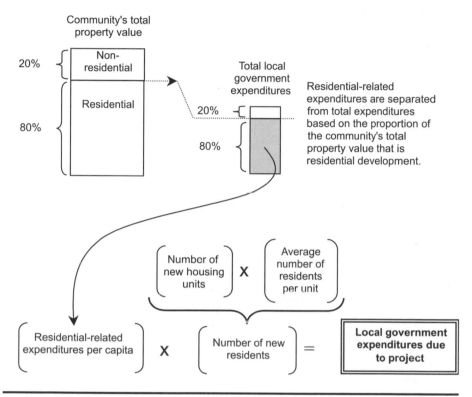

ual steps of the per capita multiplier method are outlined in Exhibit 3-26.

Case Study Method

The case study method estimates the costs of a project to a local government by systematically interviewing local government departments. The purpose of the interviews is to determine whether local government departments have excess or deficient public service capacity. Excess capacity means that a government's capacity to provide services is significantly greater than what is necessary to accommodate the existing population. Deficient capacity means just the opposite. Identifying the specific areas of a local government where excess or deficiency exists can help provide a detailed picture of the effect that an additional demand on service will have on the government. For example, a new subdivision that adds 1,000 new residents to a community may require

---

EXHIBIT 3-26 ■ Steps to the Per Capita Multiplier Method

1. Convert the total property value of the community and the total residential property value from assessed values to equalized (i.e., market or appraised) property values. Use the formula below to convert assessed values to equalized value:

$$\text{Equalized property value} = \frac{\text{Assessed property value}}{\text{Local equalization ratio}}$$

2. Calculate the residential-related expenditures per capita.
    a. Calculate the proportion of a community's total property value that is residential.

$$\frac{\text{Total residential property value}}{\text{Total community property value}} = \text{Proportion residential}$$

    b. Use the formula below.

$$\left(\begin{array}{c}\text{Residential-related}\\\text{expenditures}\end{array}\right) = \left(\begin{array}{c}\text{Total local government}\\\text{expenditures}\end{array}\right) \times \left(\begin{array}{c}\text{Proportion}\\\text{residential}\end{array}\right)$$

    c. Divide residential-related expenditures by the current population to calculate the residential-related expenditures per capita.
3. Determine the number of new residents due to the proposed project.
    a. Determine the average number of residents for the type of housing units in the proposed project. The U.S. Census Bureau website, "www.census.gov", is a convenient source of data on the average number of residents for various types of housing units.
    b. Multiply the number of new housing units by the average number of residents for that type of housing unit.
4. Estimate the total local government costs due to the proposed project by multiplying the residential-related expenditures per capita by the number of new residents.
5. Estimate the total local government revenue due to the proposed project.
6. Calculate the net fiscal impact of the proposed development by subtracting the local government cost from the revenue due to the project.

---

a large increase in fire department expenditures if the fire department does not have enough vehicles to service the existing population. However, the police department may require minimal additional expenditures if it currently has excess capacity. In this case, projecting the same percentage increase in expenditures in all government departments would underestimate the impact on the fire department and overestimate the impact on the police department.

The case study method involves seven basic steps. In the first four steps, the analyst uses interviews[24] to determine the expansion in local

---

24. Several techniques can increase the effectiveness of these interviews. Interviews should be scheduled well in advance. The interviews should be brief, and a list of written questions should be submitted before the interview. The location of the proposed development should be described accurately when interviewing local officials, as the location will determine whether existing public infrastructure can service the development.

EXHIBIT 3-27 ■ Steps to the Case Study Method

1. Initiate contact with local officials. The objectives of this step are to:
   - Gain the support of key officials (such as the city manager or administrator)
   - Obtain initial information on excess or deficient service capacity;
   - Agree on an approach for contacting and interviewing department heads; and,
   - Establish a solid working relationship with those to be interviewed.
2. Interview local officials to determine whether there are excesses or deficiences in service capacity.
3. Estimate the local government costs due to the project using simple population multipliers.
4. Reinterview local government officials to determine how their department will respond to the increased demand for services caused by the project. Use the rough estimates of local government costs calculated in step three and the knowledge of excess or deficient capacity obtained in step two to increase the accuracy of departmental estimates.
5. Convert officials' estimates of personnel, equipment, and facilities into an expenditure figure.
6. Estimate the total local government revenue due to the proposed project.
7. Calculate the net fiscal impact of the proposed development by subtracting the local government cost from the revenue due to the project.

Adapted from: *The Fiscal Impact Guidebook: Estimating Local Costs and Revenues of Land Development*, Department of Housing and Urban Development, Washington, DC: U.S. Government Printing Office, 1979, Exhibit 3-1.

---

government services that would be necessary to accommodate a proposed development. In the fifth step, this expansion is converted into an expenditure figure. The projected revenues are estimated in the sixth step. In the final step, the cost is subtracted from the revenues to calculate the net fiscal impact of the project. Each step is discussed briefly in Exhibit 3-27.

The case study method produces the most accurate and detailed analysis of fiscal impacts, but it is also the most time consuming method. In fact, a case study analysis typically takes three to four times longer than other fiscal impact analysis methods. For this reason, it should *not* be used when time for an analysis is short or when multiple alternatives are being evaluated. Because of the case study method's accuracy and detail, it is best suited for unusual nonresidential developments, such as a sports complex or convention center, that will place an unusual demand on services.

Service Standard Method

The service standard method calculates the fiscal impact of a proposed project by determining the number of government employees that a project will require, and then multiplying this by the average expenditure per employee. This method is given the name *service standard* be-

EXHIBIT 3-28 ■ A Simplified Version of the Service Standard Method

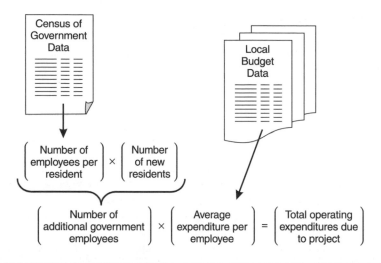

cause it uses Census data on the average number of government employees per resident as a type of industry standard for the number of employees that a government should have for particular government services. The diagram in Exhibit 3-28 illustrates the basic calculation.

The service standard method has five steps. The first step uses Census data to determine the number of additional government employees that a proposed development will require. The second step uses local budget data to estimate the average expenditure per government employee. The remaining steps calculate the total government expenditures, revenues, and net fiscal impact due to the proposed development (see Exhibit 3-29).

As an example to illustrate the service standard method, suppose a small city is evaluating a proposal to build a multistory condominium complex. The city's current population is 60,000 and the proposed development would add 300 new residents to the community. The city uses the worksheet in Exhibit 3-30 to estimate that the 300 new residents will generate approximately $570,000 in additional expenditures. The city estimated that the 300 new residents would generate approximately $650,000 in additional revenue. Subtracting the additional expenditures from the additional revenue due to the project produces a positive net fiscal impact of $80,000.

EXHIBIT 3-29 ▪ Steps to the Service Standard Method

1. Determine the number of additional government employees needed due to the project.

    a. For each major government service area, determine the average number of government employees per resident for a comparable government. The U.S. Census Bureau website, "www.census.gov", is a convenient source of data on state and local government employment per capita.

    b. Determine the number of new residents due to the proposed project. First, determine the average number of residents for the type of housing units in the proposed project. The U.S. Census Bureau website, "www.census.gov", is a convenient source of data on the average number of residents for various types of housing units. Second, multiply the average number of residents for that type of housing unit by the number of new housing units.

    c. Multiply the average number of government employees per resident by the number of new residents due to the project to calculate the number of additional government employees needed due to the project.

5. Determine the average expenditure per employee by using local budget data. For each of the major government service areas, divide the expenditure for that area by the number of employees in that area.

6. Calculate the expenditures for each major service area by multiplying the number of additional government employees by the average expenditure per employee.

7. Estimate the total local government revenue due to the proposed project.

8. Calculate the net fiscal impact of the proposed development by subtracting the local government cost from the revenue due to the project.

Selecting Appropriate Fiscal Impact Methods

This section provides a guide to selecting appropriate fiscal impact analysis methods. Because of limitations in the accuracy of the methods, it is preferable to use more than one method to estimate fiscal impact. Selecting the most appropriate fiscal impact methods depends on:

- The characteristics of the project;
- The characteristics of the local government; and,
- The time and resources available for an analysis.

Characteristics of the Project

The appropriate fiscal impact analysis method will depend on whether a project is residential or non-residential or is unusually large. The most appropriate methods for evaluating *residential* developments are the simplified per capita cost, per capita multiplier, and service standard methods. The case study method can be used to evaluate both residential and nonresidential developments. Projects that are very large and place an unusual demand on government services should be evaluated

EXHIBIT 3-30 ■ **Worksheet for Using the Service Standard Method to Calculate Municipal Cost of a Proposed Project**

Steps	Source of data	General Government	Public Safety	Community Development	Public Utilities, Parks & Recreation, and Public Works
		Government Service Functions			
A Number of Full Time Employees per capita	Census	0.00228	0.00374	0.00136	0.00325
B Expected Increase in Population Due to Project	Local estimate	300	300	300	300
C Number of New Employees Due to Project	A x B	0.68	1.12	0.41	0.98
D Current Local Expenditures for Service Functions	Local data	$13,274,463	$26,411,865	$9,236,530	$23,482,758
E Current Number of Employees	Local data	234	99	88	119
F Average Expenditures Per Employee	D ÷ E	$56,680	$266,787	$105,560	$197,334
G Additional Expenditures Due to Project	C x F	$38,769	$299,334	$43,069	$192,401

TOTAL: $573,573

with the case study method. The other methods are most accurate when the project is not unusual in scope.

Characteristics of the Local Government

A slack or deficiency in capacity to provide government services is another factor that will influence which method should be used. A project such as a new subdivision development will result in additional costs to the government in terms of additional police, fire, and other government services. If the government does not have a substantial excess or deficiency in its capacity to provide services, and the development will not require a substantial expansion in service, then the government can assume that the unit costs of providing services for the subdivision will be about the same as the unit costs of providing services to the existing population. In this scenario, the simplified per capita cost, per capita multiplier, and service standard methods should be used because these methods assume that the unit cost of providing services with a project will be about the same as the current unit cost of providing services.

However, in some cases, a project will change a government's unit costs of providing services. This will occur in two instances:

1. When a government has severe excess or deficiency in service capacity or
2. When a project is large enough that it substantially increases the size of the population.

When a government has severe excess in capacity, an additional demand for service will actually reduce unit costs because the existing services are spread over more residents. When government has a severe deficiency in capacity, an additional demand for service will increase unit costs because the government will have to substantially increase its facilities and personnel to meet the demand. If a project is large enough that it substantially increases the size of the population, the project will increase a government's unit cost of providing services because the government will have to make additional capital expenditures to meet the population increase. For example, a government may need to purchase an additional fire engine or build a new fire station. In these cases where a project significantly changes a government's unit costs of providing services, the case study method should be used because it is sensitive to changes in unit costs.

Time Available for Analysis

All of the fiscal impact methods discussed here, except for the case study method, provide relatively fast estimates of fiscal impact. The case study method is the most time consuming, and requires the most skill, but it also provides the most detailed and accurate estimate of impact. In addition to estimating the overall impact of a proposed project, the case study method also provides detailed information on the specific personnel and facility expansions that will have to be made once a project is accepted. Thus, the case study method provides information that is useful even after a decision has been made. The faster methods should be used when little time is available for an analysis or when multiple alternatives will be evaluated. Since the case study method is very

EXHIBIT 3-31 ▪ Fiscal Impact Methods

Method	Government Characteristics		Best Suited for Analyzing These Types of Projects	Advantages	Disadvantages
	Status of Government's Existing Service Quality	Population Growth Rate			
Per Capita Multiplier	• No significant excess or deficiency in capacity (typically: suburban metropolitan area municipalities, 10,000–50,000 population, and 2-3% growth rate.)	Stable to Moderate	• Residential development • Annexation • Rezoning • Evaluating landuse alternatives within a proposed growth strategy	• Quick, inexpensive, and easily implemented • Can be used to evaluate multiple alternatives	• Lacks detailed view of impact • Ignores existing service slack or deficiency
Case Study	• Any capacity including significant excess or deficiency in capacity (typically: central cities with declining population, small cities with rapid population growth)	Any	• Residential development • Traditional nonresidential development • Unusual nonresidential development that will place a unusual demand on services (e.g., sports complex, convention center)	• Avoids over or underestimating the costs of expanding service due to a government's excess or deficiency in capacity. • Provides very detailed information • Most accurate method of forecasting short term costs	• Time consuming • Expensive • Requires much skill to implement effectively
Service Standard	• No significant excess or deficiency in capacity	Stable to Moderate	• Residential development • Annexation • Rezoning • Evaluating landuse alternatives within a proposed growth strategy (Evaluated projects should *not* significantly change population growth rate.)	• Quick, inexpensive, and easily implemented • Can be used to evaluate multiple alternatives • Provides detailed information	• Ignores existing service slack or deficiency

Source: *The Fiscal Impact Guidebook: Estimating Local Costs and Revenues of Land Development,* U.S. Department of Housing and Urban Development, 1979.

time-consuming, it should not be used to evaluate multiple alternatives. Exhibit 3-31 compares fiscal impact analysis methods.

Limitations of Tool

A limitation of fiscal impact analysis is that it only considers the financial costs to the local government. It does not consider monetary or non-monetary costs and benefits to residents, and does not consider any costs and benefits to surrounding communities. Some developments, such as a shopping mall, may have important costs and benefits that are not captured in a fiscal impact analysis. For example, a shopping mall may provide residents with the benefit of time savings because stores are more conveniently located. A mall may also generate a cost to residents in terms of increased local traffic and less green space.

TOOL 11: COST-EFFECTIVENESS ANALYSIS

A cost-effectiveness analysis calculates the unit cost of a particular benefit such as the cost per life saved or the cost per can of trash collected. The primary use of a cost-effectiveness analysis is to compare alternatives to determine which alternative produces the greatest benefit at the lowest cost.

Basically, cost-effectiveness analysis puts alternatives into a form in which they can be readily compared. For example, let's say that a suburban government is comparing alternatives for refuse collection. One company will charge $129,000 for every 1,500 homes, a second company will charge $36,000 for every 500 homes, and a third company will charge $255,000 for all of the town's 3,750 homes. Because the offers are so different, they are difficult to compare. A cost-effectiveness analysis can make a comparison possible by converting all three price quotes into a similar form. This is done in Exhibit 3-32.

The cost-effectiveness analysis reveals that Company C has the best offer because it can provide refuse collection services at an annual cost of $68 per home.

Like any other tool, cost-effectiveness analysis is useful for particular types of decisions, but inappropriate for other types of decisions. As mentioned earlier, its primary use is to compare alternatives to determine which alternative can generate the greatest benefit at the least cost.

EXHIBIT 3-32 ■ A Cost-Effectiveness Analysis

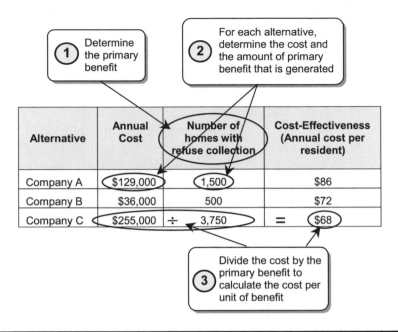

However, it cannot determine whether the benefits of a project are greater than the costs. To do this, a cost-benefit analysis should be used.

A key advantage of cost-effectiveness analysis is that it is simpler to perform than cost-benefit analysis because it is not necessary to determine *all* of the costs and benefits that a project will generate, but only the *primary* benefit of the project and its monetary costs. A project may produce many costs and benefits, but it may only be worth considering its primary benefit and monetary cost. For example, let's say that a city is considering alternative railroad crossing gates. A railroad-crossing gate may produce benefits such as time saved by train commuters due to fewer train accidents and lower accident costs to train operators. However, the *primary* benefit is lives saved. A crossing gate may also generate costs such as increased noise and traffic congestion, but these are unavoidable. Rather than attempting to calculate all of the costs and benefits that the railroad crossing gate will produce for society, it is better to simplify the analysis by only considering the primary benefit and the monetary cost. As a general rule, a cost-effectiveness analysis is probably a better tool when a project or decision is small in scope or has a primary benefit or single criteria that dominates the decision. Like-

EXHIBIT 3-33 ■ Deciding Between Cost-Effectiveness Analysis and Cost-Benefit Analysis

Use cost-effectiveness analysis when:	Use cost-benefit analysis when:
1. The decision/project is small in scope. 2. The decision/project has one primary benefit. 3. Nonmonetary costs can be ignored. 4. It is very difficult to put a dollar value on intangible benefits. 5. The benefit will be provided regardless of the decision.	1. The decision/project is large is scope. 2. The decision/project has multiple benefits or criteria that are important. 3. Nonmonetary costs cannot be ignored. 4. It is necesary to know whether the benefits of a project are greater than the costs.

wise, cost-effectiveness analysis should not be used when a decision has multiple criteria or when many different types of benefits are important. In addition, cost-effectiveness analysis should not be used when non-monetary costs are important.

A cost-effectiveness analysis is also simpler to perform than cost-benefit analysis because it does not require placing a dollar figure on intangible benefits (such as saving a human life) that are difficult to monetarize. Much effort is required to place a dollar figure on intangible benefits and the result many times is a questionable valuation. This can be avoided by using a cost-effectiveness analysis instead of a cost-benefit analysis. As a general rule, cost-effectiveness analysis is a more appropriate tool than cost-benefit analysis when it is very difficult to put a dollar value on the intangible benefits of a program.

As another general rule, a cost-effectiveness analysis is probably the better tool when a benefit will be provided regardless of the decision. For example, residents will always be provided with running water and refuse collection services, so it does not make sense to try to place a dollar figure on the benefit of having running water or having one's refuse collected as though these benefits might be taken away if the costs are greater than the benefits. The real issue is not whether the cost of running water is greater than the benefits, but what is the most inexpensive way of providing quality drinking water. Exhibit 3-33 summarizes the general rules for deciding when to use cost-effectiveness and cost-benefit analysis.

There are two primary ways that cost-effectiveness analysis can be used. The first is to determine the lowest cost alternative. The second is to determine the most effective or highest quality alternative.

EXHIBIT 3-34 ▪ Determining the Lowest Cost Alternative

Alternative	Annual Cost	Primary Benefit (Number of homes with refuse collection)	Cost-Effectiveness (Cost ÷ Primary Benefit) (Annual cost per resident)
Company A	$129,000 ÷	1,500	= $86
Company B	$36,000	500	$72
Company C	$255,000	3,750	$68

Determining the Lowest Cost Alternative

One way that cost-effectiveness analysis can be used is to determine the alternative that produces the greatest benefit at the lowest cost. This is appropriate when a unit of benefit generated by one alternative is the same as a unit of benefit provided by any other alternative. For example, a refuse container emptied by one company is the same as a refuse container emptied by any other company. The key consideration in this type of decision is which company can empty containers at the lowest cost. In these types of decisions, the following procedure can be used to determine the lowest cost alternative.

1. Determine the primary benefit to be achieved (e.g., vehicles serviced, trash collected, water purified).
2. Set the minimum standard of quality for the primary benefit (e.g., life saved and in good health, trash collected weekly at the curb, water purified to the state health standard).
3. Eliminate all alternatives that do not meet the minimum standard.
4. Evaluate each alternative using a table similar to the one in Exhibit 3-34. List each alternative in the first column. For each alternative list the cost and the amount of primary benefit that is produced. Divide the cost by the primary benefit to calculate the cost per unit of benefit.
5. Select the alternative with the lowest cost per unit of benefit.

EXHIBIT 3-35 ■ Determining the Most Effective Alternative

Budget Decision Package	Primary Benefit	Annual Cost	Benefit per $100 (Primary Benefit ÷ Cost) × 100
Teen Employment Program	800 teens employed	$40,000/yr.	2 teens employed
Youth Sports League	4,000 youth participate	$50,000/yr.	10 youth in sports leagues
Staffing for Children's Library	270,000 book checkouts	$90,000/yr.	300 books checked out

Determining the Most Effective or Highest Quality Alternative

The second way that cost-effectiveness analysis can be used is to determine the most effective or highest quality alternative. This application is appropriate when the costs of alternative projects are the same and only the benefits need to be compared. For example, when an amount has been budgeted for a project, the same budgeted amount will be spent regardless of which alternative is chosen. In these types of decisions, use the following procedure to determine the most effective or highest quality alternative.

1. Determine the primary benefit to be achieved (e.g., vehicles serviced, trash collected, water purified).
2. Determine the allowable budget for the program.
3. Eliminate all alternatives that exceed the budget.
4. Evaluate each alternative using a table similar to the one in Exhibit 3-35. List each alternative in the first column. For each alternative, list the amount of primary benefit that is produced and the cost. Divide the primary benefit by the cost to calculate the benefit per dollar.
5. Select the alternative with the highest benefit per dollar.

To illustrate how to use cost-effectiveness analysis to determine the most effective alternative, suppose a village government is considering the best use of a one-time $500,000 state grant earmarked for youth and teen programs. This funding may be used over several years. The village's community services department presents the budget director with three options:

1. A new teen employment program
2. A new youth sports league; and
3. Funding the staffing for a new children's area of the village library.

Using estimates made by the community services department, the budget director performs the cost-effectiveness analysis in Exhibit 3-35. The fourth column of this cost-effectiveness analysis shows the amount of benefit that each option can generate for each $100 of grant funds.

Limitations of Tool

Cost-effectiveness analysis cannot determine whether the benefits of an alternative are greater than the costs. As discussed earlier, its primary use is to determine which alternative can generate the greatest benefit at the least cost. Cost-effectiveness analysis is also an inappropriate tool when multiple benefits or criteria are important, or when non-monetary costs cannot be ignored.

TOOL 12: SENSITIVITY ANALYSIS

Sensitivity analysis tests how sensitive an analysis is to changes in the underlying assumptions of the analysis. There are three main methods of conducting a sensitivity analysis:

1. Recalculate the result of an analysis in a pessimistic, expected, and optimistic scenario;
2. Recalculate the result of an analysis many times by testing each uncertain assumption over a wide range of values; and,
3. Calculate a probability distribution for the result of an analysis.

To use the first method of sensitivity analysis, first list all of the assumptions that are uncertain. Second, give a pessimistic, expected, and optimistic value for each assumption. Third, test the effect that the pessimistic and optimistic values have on the total net benefit. Testing the effect of pessimistic and optimistic scenarios involves recalculating the total net benefit many times. Each time the total net benefit is recalculated, one of the assumptions is changed to an optimistic or pessimistic value while the remaining assumptions are given their expected values. This process is continued until all of the assumptions have been tested for their optimistic and pessimistic values. The result of these calcula-

EXHIBIT 3-36 ■ The Output of a Sensitivity Analysis

Only one pessimistic or optimistic value is used for each recalculation. (Shaded cells are not used in calculation.)

Uncertain Assumptions	Pessimistic Scenario	Expected Scenario	Optimistic Scenario
Population growth	0%		
GDP		3.2%	
Short term interest rates		5.2%	
State grants		$5 mil.	

Recalculation using pessimistic GDP

Recalculation using pessimistic interest rate

Recalculation using pessimistic state grant estimate

Additional recalculations generate the table below

Sensitivity Analysis of Fund Balance Estimate

Uncertain Assumptions		Pessimistic Scenario	Expected Scenario	Optimistic Scenario
Population growth	Estimate of assumption	0%	3%	5%
	Estimate of fund balance	$32,759,216	$42,182,167	53,574,832
GDP	Estimate of assumption	1.0%	3.2%	4.3%
	Estimate of fund balance	$36,186,435	$42,182,167	$45,535,541
Short term interest rates	Estimate of assumption	4.1%	5.2%	6.5%
	Estimate of fund balance	$38,765,215	$42,182,167	$44,215,535
State government grant	Estimate of assumption	$0	$5 mil.	$10 mil.
	Estimate of fund balance	$37,598,485	$42,182,167	$52,182,167

EXHIBIT 3-37 ■ Expected Value for Each Uncertain Assumption

Uncertain Assumptions	Expected Value
Discount Rate	5%
Value of time	50% of average hourly wage
Users per day	12,500

tions should reveal the assumptions to which the analysis is most sensitive, as illustrated in Exhibit 3-36.

A slightly different method of sensitivity testing involves more calculations, but shows how pessimistic an assumption would have to be to produce a certain result, such as a negative total net benefit, or a negative fund balance. In this second method of sensitivity testing, each assumption is tested over a range of many values with the expected value in the middle of the range. The procedure of sensitivity testing is the same as in method one, except instead of three values for each assumption, a range of many values is tested.

To illustrate the usefulness of this method of sensitivity testing, suppose a county government has recently conducted a cost-benefit analysis of a commuter mass transit system. Proponents have argued that a mass transit system is worth the cost because it will save commuters much travel time. In fact, the cost-benefit analysis revealed that the project has a positive total net benefit of $30 million. Before presenting a recommendation before the county board, the finance director would like information on the certainty of their estimate of a positive total net benefit, so he asks a budget analyst to perform a sensitivity analysis. The analyst identifies three uncertain assumptions in the analysis. Each of these assumptions and their expected value is listed in Exhibit 3-37.

Using spreadsheet software, the analyst recalculates the total net benefit using a wide range of values for each assumption to discover the point at which each assumption will produce a negative total net benefit, as illustrated in Exhibit 3-38.

Through this analysis, the finance director discovers that the mass transit project has a positive total net benefit for a broad range of assumptions. Another word for describing this condition is that the result

EXHIBIT 3-38 ■ Total Net Benefit Using a Range of Values for Each Assumption

Uncertain Assumptions	Scenarios	Total Net Benefit
Discount rate	0%	$56 mil.
	2.5%	$42 mil.
	5%	$30 mil.
	7.5%	$12 mil.
	10%	$4 mil.
Value of time	0% of wage	−$3 mil.
	25% of wage	$18 mil.
	50% of wage	$30 mil.
	75% of wage	$41 mil.
	100% of wage	$53 mil.
Users per day	4,000	−$2 mil.
	8,000	$12 mil.
	12,500	$30 mil.
	16,000	$34 mil.
	20,000	$37 mil.

is *robust*, that is, the result stays about the same despite a wide range of changes to the assumptions.

The third method of sensitivity analysis, simulation, is the most sophisticated. It requires statistical software and more complete data on each assumption. The great advantage of this method is that the total result of an analysis is shown as a value with a probability distribution.

To see the advantage of displaying results with a probability distribution, suppose a city is deciding between spending capital funds on a new fire station with an expected net benefit of $5 million or a parking garage with an expected net benefit of $10 million. Apparently, the parking garage is the better project because it has a greater expected net benefit. However, if the $5 million estimate is more certain than the $10 million estimate, then the fire station could be a better option.

To see how this could be, it is important to understand the concept of a probability distribution. In the example, the city calculated $10 mil-

EXHIBIT 3-39 ■ A Probability Distribution

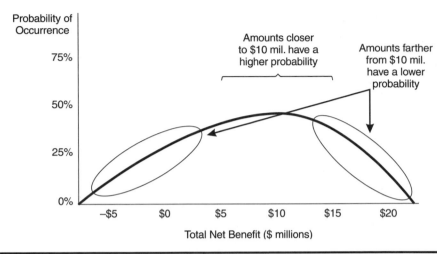

lion as the most likely estimate, however, there is a possibility that the actual amount will be lower or higher than that amount. Amounts closer to $10 million will have a higher probability and amounts further from $10 million will have a lower probability. This can be represented graphically by a distribution curve, as shown in Exhibit 3-39.

In Exhibit 3-39, the estimate of $10 million has a broad distribution. Suppose the $5 million estimate for the fire station has a narrow distribution because there is little uncertainty in the estimate. Placed together, the distributions of the two estimates are illustrated in Exhibit 3-40.

Notice that a significant portion of the distribution around the estimate for the parking garage is less than $0, while *none* of the distribution of the estimate for the fire station is below $0.

Limitations of Tool

The main drawback of simulation is that it has very high data and analysis requirements. This technique requires specialized statistical software. In addition, the analyst must have sufficient data to determine the probability distributions around estimates.

EXHIBIT 3-40 ■ **Comparison Between the Distribution of Two Estimates**

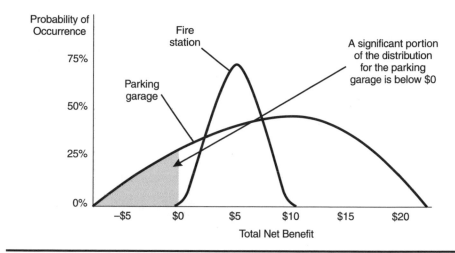

CHAPTER 4

Simplifying Decision Making

Financial decisions must often be made under a tight time constraint. Often, decision makers do not have the luxury of spending days or even hours on an analysis. This chapter addresses this issue by introducing four methods of simplifying decisions and discussing potential pitfalls to avoid when making a "gut decision."

METHODS FOR SIMPLIFYNG DECISIONS

Some decisions must be made quickly and cannot afford the time required to conduct a comprehensive analysis. Other decisions require a comprehensive analysis, but time and effort could be saved if the analysis is focused only on the most important criteria or the best alternatives. This section presents four methods of simplifying decisions and focusing an analysis only on the key criteria or alternatives.

Canceling Out Criteria

This method simplifies decisions by eliminating criteria for which the alternatives are not significantly different. Once the criteria are eliminated, the analysis can be directed to the remaining criteria. This method is most useful for decisions with few alternatives but many criteria. Exhibit 4-1 shows an example of canceling out criteria to simplify

EXHIBIT 4-1 ■ Canceling Out Criteria

	Alternatives	
Criteria	A	B
Cost	$350,000	$210,000
Customer Support	5	5
Speed	8	4
Implementation	7	8
Functionality	8	9
Ease of Use	4	7

a decision. Three of the criteria are eliminated because both alternatives have similar scores for these criteria.

Eliminate Alternatives by Criteria

This method simplifies decisions by reducing the number of alternatives. In this method, all alternatives that do not meet a minimum requirement are eliminated.

To use this method, list each criterion as a separate row and each alternative as a separate column. List the minimum requirement for each criterion in the second column. Look across the row of each criterion and eliminate any alternatives from consideration that do not meet a minimum requirement. Exhibit 4-2 illustrates how to use this method. In this illustration, two alternatives are eliminated because they do not meet the minimum requirement.

EXHIBIT 4-2 ■ Eliminate Alternatives by Criteria

Criteria	Minimum Requirement	Alternatives				
		A	B	C	D	E
Cost	< $300	$250	$500	$200	$230	$280
Reliability	> Fair	Good	Excellent	Good	Good	Good
Location	< 15 min. drive	2 min.	8 min.	5 min.	10 min.	30 min.
Customer Support	> Fair	Good	Good	Good	Good	Excellent
Average Response Time	< 2 days	1 day	6 hours	1.5 days	1 day	1 day

EXHIBIT 4-3 ■ Satisficing

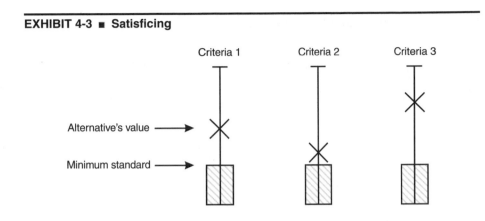

Satisficing

This method of simplifying decisions is to choose the first alternative that satisfies a minimum standard for all criteria (see Exhibit 4-3). This method is most useful for decisions that must be made quickly. In some decisions, the benefit that might be gained by selecting the very best alternative does not justify the analysis required to find that alternative. Ordering from a restaurant menu is a good illustration of this decision rule. Unless you have a lot of time on your hands, it is impractical to analyze every item on the menu and compare it to every other item. Usually, a person will select the first item that meets a few minimum criteria such as a reasonable price and a good taste.

This decision rule is also useful when alternatives must meet numerous minimum requirements and when meeting all of the requirements is more important than exceeding a few requirements. An example of this would be a decision between pollution control systems to meet federal and state mandates.

Select Alternatives Based on Most Important Criteria

Another method of simplifying a decision is to select the alternative that has the best value for the most important criteria. This method is most appropriate for decisions that must be made quickly, and for decisions for which one criteria is very important. For example, when deciding between suppliers of commodities such as fuel or paper, the decision could be simplified to selecting the supplier with the lowest price. In another example, if a government was in desperate need of a particular

EXHIBIT 4-4 ▪ Selecting Alternatives Based on the Most Important Criteria

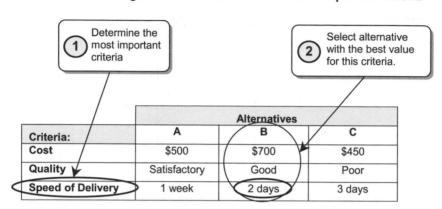

item, then the decision could be simplified to selecting the supplier with the fastest delivery speed. Exhibit 4-4 illustrates this method.

USING A "GUT FEELING" TO MAKE FINANCIAL DECISIONS

A "gut feeling" usually refers to a decision maker's intuitive sense. Although a gut feeling is not the result of a logical argument or a mathematical formula, some decision makers may unconsciously use a logical decision method and memory of past experiences to form their gut feeling.

The advantage of using a gut feeling is that decisions can be made quickly and require no analysis. In addition, a gut feeling can potentially combine several decision-making methods and lessons from past experiences.

A weakness of the logical decision methods discussed in previous chapters is that they can sometimes provide a poor recommendation when some criteria cannot be quantified or if incorrect information is used. For example, let's say that a city government is evaluating economic development programs. It uses a net present value (NPV) analysis and a discount rate of 1.5 percent to evaluate three potential programs. The NPV analysis indicates that the city would reap substantial net benefits with any of the three programs. Despite this recommendation, the city decides to reject all three programs. The decision tool did not provide the correct recommendation because the discount rate that was used did not reflect the community's strong preference for present versus future consumption. A strong preference for present consumption would be reflected by a high discount rate. However, the city used a relatively low discount rate in its analysis. A gut feeling can avoid this type of weakness of logical decision methods because a gut feeling boils down a decision to its most crucial elements and tends to correctly specify important criteria.

Problems with Relying on a Gut Feeling

For many financial decisions, a gut feeling may be the most effective method for deciding between alternatives. As discussed above, it can be a fast and effective method. Several drawbacks exist, however, to relying on intuition to make decisions.

One significant drawback is that it is highly dependent on a decision maker's personal experience and judgment. A gut feeling could work well for one person who has good judgement and poorly for another person who exercises bad judgment. Since a gut feeling is dependent on a person's personal experience, a recent, unusual experience could bias judgment and result in a bad decision. For example, a recent earthquake could influence a decision maker to make expenditures for emergency equipment that would have been considered unnecessary before the event. In contrast, a logical decision method, such as the net present value tool, has less of a chance of being biased by a person's subjective experience. Logical decision methods avoid bias by forcing a decision maker to think about each individual element in a decision.

Another drawback of relying on intuition to make a decision is that others cannot evaluate the decision process. Logical decision methods enable more than one person to evaluate the assumptions that are used to arrive at a decision.

Common Mistakes in Financial Decisions

It is useful to be aware of several common mistakes that can occur in the decision-making process:

- Cognitive illusions;
- Failure to recognize the time value of money;
- Failure to recognize opportunity cost; and
- Counting sunk costs.

A discussion of each of these *decision pitfalls* follows.

Decision Pitfall 1: Cognitive Illusions

A cognitive illusion occurs when human intuition is "tricked" into misjudging the probability of an event. In most decisions, the decision makers cannot rely on statistical analysis to determine the probability of events. Instead, they must use a simple estimating technique to make an educated guess. Human beings commonly use three techniques to estimate probabilities. Although each of these techniques works well in most situations, they fail repeatedly in particular situations. Understanding why can help to improve decision making. The following paragraphs describe each estimating technique and how it can fail.[1]

Estimating likelihood based on the extent to which an event resembles another event. One method that decision makers commonly use to estimate the probability of a future event is to compare it with a past event that it resembles and then predict a similar outcome.

A problem with this method occurs when decision makers base their decision about a future event entirely on its resemblance to a particular past event and ignore probability data on the future event. For example, a government that is considering whether a new financial system will be implemented successfully might place a low probability on success if the new system resembles a previous system that was poorly implemented. In such a situation, decision makers might tend to ignore information showing how the new system was implemented successfully in 85 percent of previous sites.[2] This is a serious error in judgment because prior probabilities should affect judgment of probability, but tend to be overshadowed by a similarity to a previous event.

Estimating likelihood based on the ease with which an event comes to mind. Another method that decision makers commonly use to estimate the probability of an event is to assign a probability to the event based on the ease with which it can be imagined. Generally, this technique can be a good method of estimating probability because events that occur more frequently (and thus have a higher probability) should

---

1. The following discussion is based on Amos Tversky and Daniel Kahneman, "Judgement Under Uncertainty: Heuristics and Biases," *Science*, 1974, volume 185, pp. 1124-1131.
2. Kahneman and Tversky proved this human tendency through psychology experiments. Daniel Kahneman and Amos Tversky, *Psychology Review*, 1973, volume 80, p. 237.

come to mind easier. However, there are cases in which this method will overestimate or underestimate the chances of an occurrence.

One case in which our intuition can be tricked into overestimating the probability of an event is when a similar, past event was very spectacular or recent. For example, travelers typically greatly overestimate the probability of being killed by an airplane crash (because it is very spectacular and can be remembered very easily), while underestimate the probability of a car accident (because it is less spectacular). Also, highway drivers may drive slower after seeing a police car on the side of the road, even though the probability of seeing another police car is not necessarily higher.

Our intuition can also be tricked when the probability of an event is estimated based on the ease with which the event can be imagined. For example, a government is unlikely to build an expensive dike for the once-in-a-lifetime flood that last occurred 100 years ago because it is difficult to imagine such a flood. A once-in-a-lifetime flood that occurred just three years ago, however, is more likely to trigger a decision to build the dike because it is easy to imagine such a flood occurring again. Ironically, the once-in-a-lifetime flood that seems unlikely to happen because it occurred so long ago is probably *more* likely to occur,

Another way that our intuition can be tricked to misestimate the probability of an event is by the tendency to assign a higher correlation between two items that are easier to associate with one another. For example, it is easy to associate an impressive and expensive downtown bank building with a bank that is unlikely to go bankrupt. Therefore, an individual may unconsciously assume a low probability of that particular bank failing, based solely on the structure's appearance.

The tendency of an initial impression to bias perception. An initial impression can also cause decision makers to make judgment errors. Psychologists have proven that people's perception tends to become anchored to their first impression, which in turn affects their prediction of the future outcome.[3] For example a budget director's evaluation of a new program will tend to remain anchored to its success or failure in its first year. If the program happened to have an extraordinarily successful first year, its evaluation would be significantly higher in successive years than if it had an extraordinarily poor first year.

Decision Pitfall 2: Failure to Recognize the Time Value of Money

The failure to recognize the time value of money is the failure to recognize that a dollar today is worth more than a dollar tomorrow. This concept is most obvious in the area of investments: $100 in cash today is worth more than a $100 savings bond that matures in 10 years. Although this concept may seem obvious, it is easy to be fooled in actual decision situations.

For example, suppose a state government is downsizing and offers to donate an old office building to a city government. After conducting a thorough analysis, the finance director recommends that the city accept the donation. The building has a 20-year lifespan, but will require a $3 million renovation in the first year, a $10 million renovation in the tenth year, and $500,000 annually for repair and maintenance costs ($200,000 more than the repair and maintenance cost for a new building). Over 20 years, the building's renovation and maintenance costs would total to $22 million. After the finance director recommends that the city accept the donation, the local papers criticize the recommendation based on the argument that the city should not dump $22 million into a run-down building when a brand new building could be purchased for only $15 million. Is this argument valid?

A net present value calculation shows that the present value of the $22 million expense over 20 years is only $14.5 million. In contrast, the present value of the cost of the new building would be $16.5 million. By recommending the old building, the finance director saved the city over $2 million.[4]

---

3. In a psychology experiment, two groups of subjects were asked to guess the percentage of African countries in the United Nations. One group was first given the number 10 percent and asked to guess how much higher or lower was the true percent. The second group was given the number 65 percent and asked the same question. The group that was given 10 percent had an average guess of 25 percent, and the group that was given 65 percent had an average guess of 45 percent. Therefore, the starting point significantly affected the estimates of both groups. P. Slovic and S. Lichtenstein, *Organizational Behavior & Human Performance*, 1971, volume 6, p. 649.

4. This calculation assumes a real discount rate of 3 percent, the maintenance costs of the new building would be $300,000 per year, and both buildings could be sold for $5 million at the end of 20 years.

Decision Pitfall 3: Failure to Recognize Opportunity Cost

The failure to recognize opportunity cost is the failure to recognize the lost opportunity of using an asset or resource in a way other than the chosen alternative. For example, if a suburban government is considering the costs of constructing a public park on vacant city property, the opportunity cost of the park would be the revenue that could have been gained if the park was sold to a developer. Therefore, the cost of the park includes not only the costs of construction and landscaping, but also the potential revenue if the land was sold. Likewise, the opportunity cost of selling the property to a developer would be the lost public recreational benefit of a park.

Decision Pitfall 4: Counting Sunk Costs

A sunk cost is one that has already occurred and will remain the same regardless of what decision is made. For this reason, sunk costs should be ignored in an analysis. One example is the fee paid to a consultant to evaluate the environmental impact of an incinerator. The fee is a sunk cost because it will remain the same regardless of whether the incinerator project is accepted or rejected.

To see how it is easy to be fooled by sunk costs, suppose a growing suburb purchased a piece of farmland for $1.8 million and spent $1.2 million to construct residential streets, sidewalks, and sewers with the expectation that it would soon be sold to a developer who would build single family homes on the site. However, six months after the infrastructure was completed, a further analysis showed that the community would be better served if a multistory apartment complex and a school were constructed on the same site. Opponents of the new plan argue that if an apartment complex and school are built on the site, the city would lose the $1.2 million it has spent on infrastructure that was designed for single family homes. Is this argument correct? Should the city include the $1.2 million it has spent on infrastructure or the $1.8 million it has spent to purchase the property in its analysis?

The answers to both questions is no. Both of these costs are sunk costs and should not be included. The $1.2 million spent on infrastructure and the $1.8 million spent to purchase the property cannot be recovered and will remain the same regardless of what decision is made. Because they are sunk costs, the cost of the property and the infrastructure should not be counted as costs in a cost-benefit analysis or other type of analysis.[5]

---

5. Even though it is a sunk cost, the $1.2 million spent on infrastructure will still affect a decision between using the site for single family homes or for an apartments/school development. The infrastructure costs of a development of single family homes will be $0 (because no infrastructure is needed), while the infrastructure costs of the apartment/school development will be the cost of converting the infrastructure to this new use.

CHAPTER 5

Using Decision Tools to Implement the NACSLB Recommended Practices

This chapter will show how decision tools can help your government to implement the recommended budget practices of the National Advisory Council on State and Local Budgeting (NACSLB), an organization established by eight state and local government associations to improve governmental budgeting. To achieve its goal, the NACSLB developed a comprehensive set of 59 recommended budget practices. These budgeting practices cover all steps of the budgeting process, including the analysis and goal setting that occurs before the written budget document is produced, the items that should be included in the budget document, and the monitoring and evaluation that occurs after the document is adopted.

The decision tools presented in this publication can help state and local governments to implement the following five budget practices:

- Practice 6.1—Develop programs and evaluate delivery mechanisms

- Practice 6.2—Develop options for meeting capital needs and evaluate acquisition alternatives

- Practice 9.4—Prepare expenditure projections

- Practice 9.5—Evaluate revenue and expenditure options
- Practice 9.6—Develop a capital improvement plan.

Each section in this chapter will summarize the main steps necessary to implement a specific budget practice and will show how decision tools can be used in these steps.

BUDGET PRACTICE 6.1—DEVELOP PROGRAMS AND EVALUATE DELIVERY MECHANISMS

This budget practice recommends that governments institute a process to develop new programs and services and review existing ones in the context of how well they meet programmatic and operating policies and plans. This process should include an examination of how a government traditionally provides the service. It also should consider whether the service could be delivered more effectively or more efficiently if provided in a different way, either by the government itself or by entities outside the government. The main steps of this practice are:

1. Develop measurable goals for the program or service that relate to the government's more general policies and plans;
2. Develop alternatives for providing the particular government service which is being evaluated;
3. Evaluate each alternative based on the cost of service, service quality and control, management issues, financial issues, impact on stakeholders, and statutory and regulatory issues; and,
4. Select the best alternative.

Using a Decision Table to Implement Practice 6.1

The third step in this practice is to evaluate alternatives based on the cost of service, service quality and control, management issues, financial issues, impact on stakeholders, and statutory and regulatory issues. The following example shows how a decision table can be used to conduct this type of evaluation.

In 1996, the City of Rock Hill, South Carolina, considered three options for providing janitorial services for city facilities. The first option was the status quo, which was to provide janitorial services in-house. The second option was to outsource janitorial services to a private janitorial company in the Rock Hill-Charlotte region. The third option was to provide janitorial services in-house, but reduce costs through reorganization.

Exhibit 5-1 shows how a decision table can be used to evaluate the three options for providing janitorial services. The first column includes 20 criteria recommended by the NACSLB for evaluating a government service. The next three columns compare the three options.

The cells in each column represent each alternative's value for each criteria. The decision table reveals that option two has the lowest direct cost (with the lowest bidder), but includes several indirect costs not shared by the other two options. Another area in which the three alternatives differ is their impact on stakeholders. Option two has the worst impact on customers and government employees, but provides a modest savings to taxpayers of $50,901 per year. Option three provides a larger savings to taxpayers, does not reduce the quality of service, and has only a small negative impact on government employees. Therefore, option three stands out as the city's best option for reducing the cost of services.[1]

Using Activity-Based Costing to Implement Practice 6.1

In order to use a decision table to evaluate program alternatives, it is necessary to have estimates of the direct and indirect costs of government programs. Activity-based costing is a useful method of estimating these costs. For example, if a city were considering privatizing the towing and disposal of abandoned vehicles, it would use activity-based costing to estimate the current cost of providing the service with city employees and vehicles. Estimating the total direct and indirect costs of the service provides a basis from which to evaluate the proposals of private vendors.[2]

Using a Cost-Effectiveness Analysis to Implement Practice 6.1

An important part of this practice is to evaluate whether a service could be delivered more effectively or more efficiently if provided in a differ-

---

1. This example is based on *1996 Budget Workshop*, City of Rock Hill, South Carolina, pp. 78-82.
2. It is also important to break down the direct and indirect costs of the service in order to identify any indirect costs which would still continue if the service is privatized (e.g., program monitoring, central finance & administration, etc.)

EXHIBIT 5-1 ■ Using a Decision Table to Implement Practice 6.1

Evaluation Criteria	Option 1: Status Quo	Option 2: Outsource	Option 3: In-house with reorganization
Cost of service			
• Direct costs	$433,175	$295,874 to $464,468	$355,626
• Cost to administer	$0	Unspecified amount	$0
• Impact on rates and charges	n/a	n/a	n/a
• Impact on costs of other government services	$0	Costs of special events and other projects may increase (*)	Save $4,200 annually in contract expenses (****)
• Other costs	$0	$ 86,400 (**)	$0
Service quality and control			
• Safety & reliability	High	Questionable	High
• Ability to control service levels and who receives service	High	Questionable	High
• Ability of government to make internal changes to improve its own performance	n/a	n/a	n/a
• Ability to change delivery mechanism in the future	High	High	High
• Risk of contractual nonperformance and default	None	Unknown	None
Management issues			
• Quality of monitoring	High	Low	High
• Reporting and performance evaluation systems	n/a	n/a	n/a
• Public access to information	n/a	n/a	n/a
• Ability to generate or sustain competition in service delivery	High	High	High
Financial issues			
• Impact on outstanding debt	n/a	n/a	n/a
• Grant eligibility	n/a	n/a	n/a
Impact on stakeholders			
• Government employees	No change	16 staff laid off	3 staff laid off; Additional workload for remaining staff
• Customers	No change	Possible reduction in cleanliness	No change
• Taxpayers	No change	Savings of $50,901	Savings of $81,749
Statutory & regulatory issues			
• Impact on Federal and state legal and regulatory requirements	n/a	n/a	n/a
• Liability	n/a	n/a	n/a
Summary of costs	$433,175	$382,274+ (***)	$351,426

Notes:

*	Current staff assists other departments with these projects.
**	$18,900 unused vacation time of laid off employees + $67,500 unemployment benefits.
***	Administrative cost and possible increased costs of special events and other projects; Potential reduction in cleanliness.
****	Janitorial staff will service the water filter plant.

EXHIBIT 5-2 ■ **Using a Cost-Effectiveness Analysis to Implement Practice 6.1**

Alternative	Cost	Number of meals annually	Cost-Effectiveness (Cost per meal)
Program A	$350,00	108,000	$3.24
Program B	$525,00	109,500	$4.79
Program C	$880,00	164,250	$5.36

ent way. Cost-effectiveness analysis is a useful tool for determining the most efficient or effective alternative for providing a government service.

In the example shown in Exhibit 5-2, a city uses cost-effectiveness analysis to evaluate three alternatives for providing hot meals to 150 homebound senior citizens. Program A provides three meals five days a week, Program B provides two meals 365 days a year, and Program C provides three meals 365 days a year. This cost-effectiveness analysis indicates that Program A is the most cost-effective alternative.

BUDGET PRACTICE 6.2—DEVELOP OPTIONS FOR MEETING CAPITAL NEEDS AND EVALUATE ACQUISITION ALTERNATIVES

This budget practice recommends that governments develop and evaluate alternatives for meeting their capital needs. Alternatives may include both public and private provision of the capital asset. Governments should have a process that identifies capital projects that are needed to achieve goals and a general time frame in which these assets will be needed. This assessment should consider need, life cycle costs (including operating costs), impact on services, beneficiaries of the project, financing issues, and other impacts. Plans for acquiring capital assets should be part of or consistent with land use, transportation, or other long-range plans of the community or area. The main steps of this practice are:

1. Identify capital assets that are needed to achieve goals and a general time frame in which these assets will be needed.

2. For each asset, assess the need for the asset, life cycle costs (including operating costs), impact on services, beneficiaries of the asset, financing issues, and other impacts.
3. Develop alternatives for providing the capital assets.
4. Evaluate each alternative based on the following considerations:

   • Costs, including both capital and operating costs, impact on rates and charges, and impact on costs of other government services;

   • Effects on service, including technical and financial capabilities of the entity that owns the asset, ability to control the use of the asset (including expanding or contracting the facility), ability to maintain the asset, and risk of contractual nonperformance and default;

   • Management issues, including maintaining oversight of the asset and related services and operations, impact on economic growth and development, impact on service coordination, and public access to information;

   • Financial issues, including availability of cash, budgetary impacts, impact on outstanding debt, and grant eligibility; and,

   • Impact on stakeholders such as government employees, customers, and taxpayers.
5. Select the best alternative.

Using a Decision Table to Implement Practice 6.2

The fourth main step in this practice is to evaluate capital alternatives based on a wide range of considerations, such as financial, political, administrative, and technical considerations. A decision table is a useful tool for this step because it provides a method of evaluating alternatives over a wide range of criteria. The example below shows how the City of Franklin, Ohio, used a decision table.

In 1995, the City of Franklin, Ohio, became the first government to privatize a wastewater treatment plant that had been constructed with federal grant funds. Before making its decision to privatize, the city evaluated three options for the ownership and maintenance of its wastewater treatment plant. The three options were: maintaining public ownership of the plant, creating a regional sewer district, and privat-

EXHIBIT 5-3 ■ **Using a Decision Table to Implement Practice 6.2**

Evaluation Criteria		Alternatives		
		Maintain Public Ownership	Regional Sewer District	Privatization
Economic Criteria	Short term rate impacts (first 5 years)	C	C-	B+
	Long term rate impacts (20 year horizon)	B+	C	B+
	Economic risks (capital expansion, flow and loading variation, regulatory changes, etc.)	B	B	B+
Non-Economic Criteria	Control by municipalities	C+	B-	C
	Regulatory compliance	B	B-	B+
	Rate stability	C	C-	A
	Quality of service	B+	B+	B+
	Responsiveness to capital expansion requests	C	B+	A-
	Public acceptance	B+	B-	B-
	Accountability	B-	B+	C+
	Public implementation of the alternative	A	C	B-

ization. The city used the decision table shown in Exhibit 5-3 to evaluate these alternatives.[3]

Using Net Present Value Analysis to Implement Practice 6.2

An important part of the fourth step of this practice is to evaluate the financial costs and benefits of capital alternatives. Net present value analysis is a useful tool to use in this evaluation. Capital alternatives typically generate costs and benefits over many years, and it is not uncommon for a capital acquisition decision to involve a choice between a "pay now" or "pay later" alternative. In order to compare these types of alternatives, it is useful to combine, into a single number, all of the benefits and costs that an alternative generates over time. This num-

---

3. This example is based on "Privatizing Wastewater Treatment in Franklin, Ohio," in *Government Finance Review*, February, 1996, pp. 36-37.

ber is the present value of an alternative's future benefits and costs. Once all of the benefits and costs of each alternative are converted into their present value, a decision maker can easily compare the alternatives and select the alternative with the highest present value.

To illustrate this, suppose a Midwestern city is evaluating three alternatives for the improvement of its public fitness center. One alternative is to renovate and maintain the existing facility that is aging and is badly in need of repairs. This alternative would entail a modest expense but over an extended period. (The facility would be sold at the end of the period.) A second alternative is to construct a new fitness facility. This would entail a large initial expense, but a smaller maintenance expense over time. (The facility would be sold at the end of the period.) A third alternative is for a private company to own and operate the facility. With this alternative, the city would receive a large initial sum from the sale of the facility, but lose many years of future revenue from membership and license fees. Exhibit 5-4 compares the benefits and costs of each alternative and each alternative's net present value. A net present value analysis shows that, at discount rate of 3 percent, Option 3 has the highest net present value.

Using Cost-Benefit Analysis to Implement Practice 6.2

Cost-benefit analysis is a useful tool for evaluating major capital decisions that are large in scope and that generate important non-monetary costs and benefits. For example, a proposal to build a dam to prevent flooding, generate electricity, and create a lake for water recreation activities would be a good candidate for a cost-benefit analysis because it would create significant monetary and non-monetary costs and benefits for the local government, its residents, and residents of surrounding communities. It would not be appropriate to use fiscal impact analysis because this type of analysis only measures the costs and benefits to the government, and this project would also have a significant impact on residents and surrounding communities. Because cost-benefit analysis is time-consuming and has a much larger scope than other tools of analysis, it is not an appropriate tool for evaluating projects that do not have a major impact on the community and surrounding areas. It is also not well suited for decisions with many alternatives because it is very time-consuming to calculate the net benefit of each alternative.

EXHIBIT 5-4 ▪ Using Net Present Value Analysis to Implement Practice 6.2

Option 1: Renovate and Maintain the Existing Facility ($000)										
		Year								
	Now	2	3	4	5	6	7	8	9	10
Benefits	$350	$350	$350	$350	$350	$350	$350	$350	$350	$1,500
Costs	–$330	–$330	–$330	–$330	–$330	–$330	–$330	–$330	–$330	–$330
Net Benefit	$20	$20	$20	$20	$20	$20	$20	$20	$20	$1,170

Net Present value = $1,121,000

Option 2: Construct a New Fitness Facility ($000)										
		Year								
	Now	2	3	4	5	6	7	8	9	10
Benefits	$350	$350	$350	$350	$350	$350	$350	$350	$350	$1,500
Costs	–$1,500	–$230	–$230	–$230	–$230	–$230	–$230	–$230	–$230	–$230
Net Benefit	–$1,150	$120	$120	$120	$120	$120	$120	$120	$120	$1,270

Net Present value = $729,000

Option 3: Privatize Facility ($000)										
		Year								
	Now	2	3	4	5	6	7	8	9	10
Benefits	$1,500	$0	$0	$0	$0	$0	$0	$0	$0	$0
Costs	–$0	–$0	–$0	–$0	–$0	–$0	–$0	–$0	–$0	–$0
Net Benefit	$1,500	$0	$0	$0	$0	$0	$0	$0	$0	$0

Net present value = $1,500,000

BUDGET PRACTICE 9.4—PREPARE EXPENDITURE PROJECTIONS

This budget practice recommends that governments prepare multi-year projections of expenditures for each fund and for existing and proposed programs. These projections should extend at least three years into the future to uncover trends, evaluate how costs may change over time, and isolate non-recurring costs or savings. Fund level and government-wide expenditure projections should be prepared and documented so that they may be linked with the accounting system and integrated into overall financial projections. All expenditure projections should identify service level assumptions and key issues that may affect actual expenditures. Assumptions for expenditure projections should be consistent with related revenue and program performance assumptions. A single expenditure projection may be prepared based on one set of assumptions (covering multiple periods); or, multiple projections using alternative sets of assumptions may be prepared in order to more clearly identify the impact of different scenarios. Fiscal impact analysis and sensitivity analysis are useful tools to implement this practice.

Using Fiscal Impact Analysis to Implement Practice 9.4

Although fiscal impact analysis is designed mainly to predict the municipal expenditures necessary to support a specific residential or commercial development, this tool can also be used to predict a local government's future expenditures due to growth. Decision tool 10 presented several fiscal impact analysis methods. To use these fiscal impact tools to predict future expenditures, treat the community's new residential development due to population growth as though it were a single project and estimate future local government residential-related expenditures using the service standard method, case study method, or per capita multiplier method.

Using Sensitivity Analysis to Implement Practice 9.4

Sensitivity analysis is a useful tool to see what affect changes in key assumptions, such as the population growth rate, will have on future expenditures. This is one aspect of budget practice 9.4, which states that governments may wish to prepare multiple projections using alternative sets of assumptions to clearly identify the impact of different scenarios on future expenditures. Sensitivity analysis is the best tool for calculating these multiple projections.

Decision tool 12 presented three methods of sensitivity analysis. The first method is the most appropriate for this budget practice because it is the simplest to use and does not generate too much information. In this method of sensitivity analysis, an analyst calculates what the future expenditures would be in the pessimistic, optimistic, and expected scenarios of each of the uncertain assumptions.

BUDGET PRACTICE 9.5—EVALUATE REVENUE AND EXPENDITURE OPTIONS

This budget practice recommends that before governments make decisions about specific programs and revenue sources, they should first consider the "big picture" of how total revenue and expenditure levels will affect the government's financial condition in the budget period and future years. The rationale for this practice is that decision makers should have an understanding of the financial implications of revenue and spending options being considered, including the ability of the government to sustain programs and services in the long run. To carry out this practice, a government should undertake a comprehensive review of options for program and service levels and projected funding amounts. This review should highlight the affect of each option on beginning and ending fund balances; changes in fund balances at a fund level, for the government as a whole, and for major programs; and outstanding debt levels. The main components of this practice are:

1. Determine whether a package of revenue and expenditure options being considered for the budget will maintain, erode, or improve a government's financial position in the budget period and longer term.
2. Consider the degree of revenue diversification.
3. Review revenues identified as one-time or unpredictable and their uses.
4. Evaluate the extent to which program fees cover program costs. This process does not necessarily involve dedicating revenues to support specific programs (other than enterprise operations). Before dedicating revenues, governments should consider any impact such action might have on financial flexibility and whether it would reduce the level of scrutiny given to program expenditures and operating efficiency.
5. Document the analysis in the budget document. Include actual and projected financial information and assumptions used for preparing projections.

Using Sensitivity Analysis to Implement Practice 9.5

The main component of this practice is to evaluate the effect that providing services and taxing at various levels will have on a government's

EXHIBIT 5-5 ■ Effect of Taxation and Service Level Options on Fund Balance

	5% Tax Cut	Tax at Same Rates	5% Tax Increase
Decrease Service Levels	$7 mil.	$9 mil.	$11 mil.
Service Levels Unchanged	$2 mil.	$4 mil.	$6 mil.
Increase Service Levels	−$3 mil.	−$1 mil.	$1 mil.

financial condition. Sensitivity analysis is a good tool for this type of analysis. After forecasting expenditures using the assumption that taxes and service levels will remain the same, a government may wish to explore the affect that increasing or lowering tax rates and increasing or decreasing service levels will have on a government's financial condition. This evaluation is basically a type of sensitivity analysis. Exhibit 5-5 shows a possible output of this type of evaluation.

In Exhibit 5-5, the columns represent three revenue options: a 5 percent tax cut, keeping taxes at previous levels, and a 5 percent tax increase. The rows represent three expenditure options: decreasing service levels, keeping service levels unchanged, and increasing service levels. The cell in the middle of the table is the status quo. This table reveals that this government could maintain a positive fund balance with a 5 percent tax cut as long as it does not increase the level of services.

BUDGET PRACTICE 9.6—DEVELOP A CAPITAL IMPROVEMENT PLAN

This budget practice recommends that governments develop a capital improvement plan (CIP) that identifies its priorities and time frame for undertaking capital projects and provides a financing plan for those projects. The plan should include both capital and operating costs, and project at least five years into the future. The main steps in developing a CIP are outlined in Exhibit 5-6[4].

---

4. The steps in Exhibit 5-6 are taken from the GFOA publication *Capital Improvement Programming: A Guide for Smaller Governments,* by Patricia Tigue, Chicago, IL: Government Finance Officers Association, 1996, p. 7. The reader should refer to this publication for a full discussion of this topic.

EXHIBIT 5-6 ■ Steps in Developing a Capital Improvement Plan

1. Establish the administrative structure.
   - Appoint a coordinating unit or individual
   - Distinguish between capital and operating expenditures
   - Determine number of years in CIP
   - Prepare calendar of key events
   - Formulate procedures for citizen input
2. Establish the policy framework.
   - Develop programmatic policies
   - Develop financial policies
3. Develop capital project evaluation criteria.
4. Prepare capital needs assessment.
   - Prepare capital inventory
   - Evaluate whether to repair or replace facilities
   - Identify future needs
5. Identify projects for capital program.
   - Review status of previously approved projects
   - Identify and develop information for new projects
   - Examine capital project alternatives
6. Undertake financial capacity analysis.
   - Evaluate financial condition
   - Assess likelihood past trends will continue

7. Evaluate funding options.
8. Evaluate and program capital projects.
   - Review project applications
   - Prioritize capital projects
   - Select projects, schedule, and assign a funding source
9. Adopt capital program and budget.
   - Prepare a CIP document
   - Submit preliminary CIP to legislative body
   - Engage in formal public hearings
   - Revise CIP and send to legislative body for adoption
10. Implement and monitor capital budget.
    - Assign a project manager
    - Refine project milestone and cost schedules
    - Prepare progress reports
    - Review progress and take corrective actions
    - Assess bond-funded projects
    - Monitor external environment
11. Evaluate CIP process.
    - Consider organizational/process issues
    - Review forms and documents
    - Examine financial assumptions and funding sources

Using Weighted Score Tables to Implement Practice 9.6

Prioritizing capital projects is an important component of step 8 of the CIP process. A weighted score table (decision tool 3), is a useful tool for prioritizing alternatives when a decision involves many criteria that differ in importance. Exhibit 5-7 provides an example of a weighted score table used to evaluate capital project alternatives. The columns of the table list each proposed capital project. The rows list the local government's criteria for evaluating capital projects. Each criterion is weighted for importance in the second column. Each capital project is given a score from 0 to 10 based on how well it meets each criterion. These scores are then multiplied by the weight of each criterion to calculate a weighted score for that criterion. These weighted scores are summed together to calculate the project's total weighted score.

Using a Decision Tree to Implement Practice 9.6

A decision tree is a useful tool for deciding between capital projects intended for emergencies. For these types of capital decisions, a decision tree can determine whether the probability of a disaster justifies the cost

EXHIBIT 5-7 ■ Using a Weighted Score Table to Prioritize Capital Project Proposals

Criteria	Weights	Alternatives					
		1. Fire Station		2. Recreational Center		3. Playground & Soccer Field	
		Score	Weighted score	Score	Weighted score	Score	Weighted score
Addresses Emergency or Public Safety Need	.9	9	8.1	3	2.7	1	.9
Corrects Deficiency in Service or Facility	.6	2	1.2	8	4.8	9	5.4
Provides Capacity Needed for Future Growth	.6	2	1.2	7	4.2	6	3.6
Results in Long-Term Cost Savings	.5	4	2.0	3	1.5	8	4.0
Total Weighted Score			12.5		13.2		13.9

of the project. In the example in Exhibit 5-8, a city uses a decision tree to decide between two flood dikes.

Dike B is more expensive than Dike A, but will protect the city from a major flood that is estimated to cause $20 million in damage. Multiplying the probabilities by the outcomes reveals that Dike A has the lowest expected cost.

Using Net Present Value Analysis to Implement Practice 9.6

Net present value analysis is most useful for evaluating long-term capital projects and financing options in which the primary considerations are financial. Some examples of decisions that are more purely financial in character include: enterprise fund projects, repair versus replacement decisions, and lease-purchase decisions. Net present value analysis would be used in step 7 and 8 of the CIP process. This tool is less useful for decisions in which political or other intangible costs and benefits are important because it relies on monetary values for all costs and benefits.

EXHIBIT 5-8 ▪ Using a Decision Tree to Implement Pratice 9.6

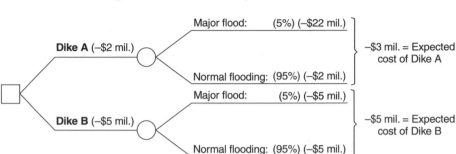

Using Return on Investment Analysis to Implement Practice 9.6

Return on investment (ROI) analysis is also a useful tool for evaluating long-term capital projects (step 8 of the CIP process). Like net present value analysis, ROI analysis is most useful for decisions in which the primary considerations are financial. ROI analysis evaluates a project's costs and benefits over time to determine the likelihood that a project will break even.

There are several rules of thumb that can be used to decide whether a net present value analysis or an ROI analysis is the most appropriate tool. ROI is a more appropriate tool than net present value analysis when the discount rate is uncertain or controversial. Unlike net present value analysis, ROI analysis calculates a capital project's net present value over a *range* of discount rates.

Net present value analysis should be used in place of ROI analysis when a project's net benefits in future years alternate from positive to negative. ROI analysis should not be used for these cases because it calculates a zero net present value at multiple discount rates.

Net present value analysis is superior to ROI analysis when the discount rate is certain and mutually exclusive alternatives are being compared. ROI analysis is not well suited for deciding between alternatives. It is possible for an alternative to break even at a higher discount rate (i.e., have a higher rate of return), but be an inferior project because it has a lower net present value at the government's discount rate.

EXHIBIT 5-9 ■ Useful Decision Tools for NACSLB Budget Practices

Budget Practice	Useful Decision Tools
6.1—Develop programs and evaluate delivery mechanisms	• Decision table • Activity-based costing • Cost-effectiveness analysis
6.2—Develop options for meeting capital needs and evaluate acquisition alternatives	• Decision table • Net present value analysis • Cost-benefit analysis
9.4—Prepare expenditure projections	• Fiscal impact analysis • Sensitivity analysis
9.5—Evaluate revenue and expenditure options	• Sensitivity analysis
9.6—Develop a capital improvement plan	• Weighted score table • Decision tree • Net present value analysis • Return on investment analysis

SUMMARY

This chapter showed how decision tools can be used to implement five NACSLB recommended practices. As a review, Exhibit 5-9 lists the tools that are useful for each practice.

CHAPTER 6

Communicating Budgetary Analysis to Decision Makers

This book has focused on how to *perform* analyses. The second half of an analyst's job is to *communicate* the results in a form that decision makers understand and find useful. Clear communication is essential for an analysis to be included in the decision-making process.

The two main tools for communicating an analysis are the *policy memo* and the *oral presentation*. A policy memo is a short, one- to three-page summary of the method and recommendations of an analysis. An oral presentation or briefing is an in-person communication of the method and recommendations of an analysis. This chapter will present some tips for both of these forms of communication.

TIPS FOR WRITING A POLICY MEMO

1. **Keep explanation of analysis simple.**[1] Simplicity is the most important rule when writing a policy memo. The methods used in an analysis should be described clearly, concisely, and with-

---

1. This discussion on writing a policy memo is based on *Public Policy Analysis: An Introduction*, by William N. Dunn, Englewood Cliffs, NJ: Prentice-Hall, Inc., 1994, pp. 423-442; and *Basic Methods of Policy Analysis and Planning*, by Carl V. Patton and David S. Sawicki, Englewood Cliffs, NJ: Prentice-Hall, Inc., 1993, pp. 134-140.

EXHIBIT 6-1 ■ Performing and Communicating Budgetary Analysis

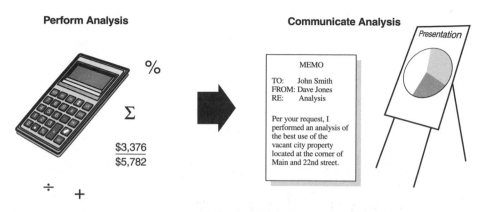

out jargon. Decision makers are most likely to follow the conclusions of an analysis that they understand and believe. To keep the explanation of an analysis simple, it is generally better to keep the analysis itself as simple as the problem allows.

2. **Double-check accuracy of analysis.** Recheck all calculations and the accuracy of the underlying data.

3. **Document assumptions and method.** Clearly documenting the assumptions and methods used adds credibility to an analysis. It also enables someone else to replicate the analysis.

4. **Report the limitations.** Report the limitations of the analysis and point out where considerable uncertainty exists in assumptions or underlying data.

5. **Use graphs and visuals.**[2] It is easier for human beings to comprehend and remember pictures than numbers and text. Three cardinal rules of graphing should be followed for a graph to have maximum impact:

   • Always explain the message of a graph "with words placed physically close to, and preferably, on the graph."[3] The analyst should not assume that a graph's message will be apparent to the viewer. The point of the graph should be stated ex-

---

2. This discussion of graphs and visuals is based on an unpublished manuscript *Using Graphs and Visuals to Present Financial Information,* by Joseph T. Kelley, and Michael C. Bestor, "Graphic Communications in a Crisis," *Government Finance Review*, October 1996, pp. 15-17.

3. Ibid.

plicitly on the graph itself. Many times this can be done with a caption pointing to a specific part of the graph.

- Always refer to the graph in the body of the text. A graph should be used to strengthen or illustrate a point that is made in the text of a memo or report.
- Polish a graph "until it has maximum message and minimum ink."[4] The *less is more* principle should be remembered when graphing financial information. Too many lines and visual effects can distract a viewer from the point of the graph and dilute the message.

Current spreadsheet software makes it simple to generate virtually any type of graph. The danger, however, is that graphs are so easy to generate that they will be done with very little thought or planning. Exhibit 6-2 presents advice on selecting an appropriate graph.

Organization of memos and reports. Analytic reports and memos can vary in format, but typically have a structure similar to that suggested in Exhibit 6-3.

4. Ibid.

EXHIBIT 6-2 ■ Selecting an Appropriate Graph

If your message is about...	Your first choice might be...	Your second choice might be...
Parts of a whole		
Time series	Many data points Few data points	Many data points
Comparisons or display with no natural order		
Comparison between two or more variables	Few data points Many data points	High low series
A cause and effect relationship		XY with trend line
Combinations (overlays) of the above	Line with columns	Area graph with columns
Numerous data points	Formatted table	Multiple columns
Quality measurement	Pareto chart	SPC chart
Interrelationships of a process	Flow chart PERT chart	Gantt chart
Dispersion of a data set	Histogram	Boxplots

Source: *Using Graphs and Visuals to Present Financial Information* (unpublished), by Joseph T. Kelley.

EXHIBIT 6-3 ■ Organizing Policy Memos and Reports

1. *Summary.* A one-page summary statement should begin the report and should devote one short paragraph to each section of the report. Next, report on each area in more detail.

2. *Problem Definition.* Describe and explain the problem using statistics, graphics, anecdotes, or other devices. Argue how the audience or client ought to perceive the problem.

3. *Evaluation Criteria.* Clarify "what is good." List and explain the criteria you used. Be sensitive to political constraints.

4. *Alternatives.* Describe the alternatives. Group similar alternatives and discuss the general types and variations.

5. *Analysis and Comparison.* Explain how you evaluated the alternatives using the criteria you have already described. Use basic statistics, decision analysis, mathematical formulas, scenarios, and other techniques you can defend. Test the sensitivity of alternatives to changes in parameters. Summarize and compare the alternatives. Exclude inadequate alternatives, after briefly and defensibly explaining why, and detail other alternatives.

6. *Conclusion.* Present your conclusions and recommendations. Report uncertainties and the effects of accepting your conclusions and following your recommendations.

7. *Next Steps.* Is more research and analysis needed? What specific steps should your client take next if your recommendations are accepted? Include plans for monitoring and evaluation. Offer alternative steps as well, to avoid forcing the client to choose all or nothing.

SOURCE: *Basic Methods of Policy Analysis and Planning*, by Carl V. Patton and David S. Sawicki, Englewood Cliffs, NJ: Prentice-Hall, Inc., 1993, p. 139.

TIPS FOR DOING AN ORAL PRESENTATION

1. **Match the communications strategy to the characteristics of the audience.** [5] The most basic step in preparing an oral presentation or briefing is to consider the audience. Some important audience characteristics to consider include:

   - The size of the audience;
   - The familiarity of the audience with analytic methods;
   - Your credibility with the audience;

---

5. This discussion on doing an oral presentation is based on *Public Policy Analysis: An Introduction*, by William N. Dunn, Englewood Cliffs, NJ: Prentice-Hall, Inc., 1994, pp. 443-446; *Basic Methods of Policy Analysis and Planning*, by Carl V. Patton and David S. Sawicki, Englewood Cliffs, NJ: Prentice-Hall, Inc., 1993, pp. 140-141; and James G. Scharret and Barbara Bartos, "Communicating Financial Information: Southfield's Financial Public Relations," *Government Finance Review*, April 1991, pp. 21-23.

- The preference of the audience for detailed or general information; and,
- Where the presentation falls in the decision-making process.

2. **Strong introduction.** Plan a strong opening that convinces listeners that the information about to be presented is something that they need to know.

3. **Summarize presentation.** Boil the presentation down to its essence and present this as a summary at the beginning of the presentation.

4. **Be clear and brief.** Keep presentation as concise as possible. "Stick to the point and cut whatever can be cut."[6]

5. **Use graphs and visuals.** (See discussion under "Tips for writing a policy memo.")

6. **Avoid jargon.** Avoid jargon and technical language that may be unfamiliar to the audience.

---

6. James G. Scharret and Barbara Bartos, "Communicating Financial Information: Southfield's Financial Public Relations," *Government Finance Review*, April 1991, p. 22.

Useful Web Sites for Financial, Economic, and Government Data

Category	Web Site
Data on the Economy and Financial Markets	**The Federal Reserve Bank of St. Louis** Contains current and historical data on interest rates, CPI, GDP, and other economic indicators. http://www.stls.frb.org/fred/
	U.S. Bureau of Labor Statistics Contains extensive data on employment, prices, and compensation. Includes useful profiles of local employment and salary data for many metropolitan areas. http://www.bls.gov/datahome.htm
	U.S. Bureau of Economic Analysis Contains data on GDP, personal income, consumption, and other data. http://www.bea.doc.gov/ The "BEA Regional Facts" section of this Web site produces computer-generated narrative profiles of states, counties, and metropolitan areas using personal income and industry data. http://www.bea.doc.gov/bea/regional/bearfacts/
	The Beige Book, The Federal Reserve Board Summarizes regional economic activity in the twelve Federal Reserve districts. Includes information on regional labor market conditions and prices. It also contains summaries of key sectors within each region such as retail trade, manufacturing, services, construction and real estate, banking and finance, and agriculture. The Beige Book provides economic information in a narrative format. It is updated every one to two months. http://www.federalreserve.gov/fomc/beigebook/2001/default.htm

Category	Web Site
Forecasts of Economic Data	**The Budget and Economic Outlook, Congressional Budget Office** Contains ten-year forecasts of GDP, CPI, unemployment, interest rates, wages and salaries, and corporate profits. http://www.cbo.gov/
	Livingston Survey, The Federal Reserve Bank of Philadelphia A bi-annual survey of 31 economists from industry, government, banking, and academia. Contains two-year forecasts of GDP, corporate profits, industrial production, producer prices, CPI, average weekly earnings, retail trade, housing starts, automobile sales, unemployment, prime rate, 3-month Treasury bill, 30-year Treasury bond, and stock prices. Also contains ten-year forecasts of the GDP and CPI. http://www.phil.frb.org/econ/liv/index.html
	Survey of Professional Forecasters, The Federal Reserve Bank of Philadelphia A quarterly survey of 34 private-sector economists. Contains two-year forecasts of GDP, CPI, unemployment, interest rates, and other major macroeconomic indicators. Also contains a ten-year forecast of the CPI. http://www.phil.frb.org/econ/spf/index.html
State and Local Government Financial Data	**Census of Governments, U.S. Census Bureau** Contains breakdowns of revenues and expenditures by major categories. Data is available for some individual governments and is aggregated by state. http://www.census.gov/govs/www/index.html
	U.S. Bureau of Economic Analysis Contains historical, aggregated data on total state and local government receipts and expenditures. http://www.bea.doc.gov/
	Federation of Tax Administrators Contains data on state tax rates and state and local government tax revenue. http://www.taxadmin.org/fta/rate/tax_stru.html
	Municipal Cost Index, American City and County Magazine Contains data on an inflation index that specifically measures inflation in the cost of municipal services. The data is updated monthly. The site includes historical values for the index since 1978. http://www.americancityandcounty.com/

Category	Web Site
Crime and Criminal Justice Data	**National Criminal Justice Reference Service, U.S. Department of Justice** A gateway to the criminal justice databases maintained by the U.S. Department of Justice. http://www.ncjrs.org/ncjover.htm
	Guide to Abstracts and Bibliographies of Data Sets on Crime and Criminal Justice, University of Texas at Austin Contains abstracts and bibliographies of studies that use U.S. Bureau of Justice statistics data sets. Contains links to federal government data sets. http://www.la.utexas.edu/research/crime_criminaljustice_research/
Education Data	**National Center for Education Statistics, U.S. Department of Education** Main gateway to U.S. federal government data on education. http://nces.ed.gov/
Data on Multiple Topics	**U.S. Census Bureau** Main gateway to U.S. Census Bureau Web site. Provides data on many subjects including: agriculture, banking, crime, education, government finances and employment, health, housing, income, population, and trade. http://www.census.gov
	Government Information Sharing Project, Oregon State University Generates tables of Census data on numerous topics aggregated by county region. All U.S. counties included. http://govinfo.kerr.orst.edu/usaco-stateis.html
	Integrated Public Use Microdata Series, University of Minnesota Combines U.S. Census data from 1850 to 1990. http://www.ipums.umn.edu/
	Web Access to *City and County Databook*, University of Virginia Library Provides access to the 1988 and 1994 versions of the City and County Databook. Provides data on many subjects including: agriculture, banking, crime, education, government finances and employment, health, housing, income, population, and trade. Data is aggregated by individual counties and cities with more than 25,000 inhabitants. http://fisher.lib.virginia.edu/ccdb/

Category	Web Site
Gateways and Lists of Web Sites with Statistical Data	**Statistical Resources on the Web, University of Michigan** An annotated list of Web sites with statistical data on a wide range of topics including: agriculture, business and industry, government finance, housing, demographics, environment, sociology, and transportation. http://www.lib.umich.edu/libhome/Documents.center/stats.html
	The Directory of Online Statistics Sources, Berinstein Research A comprehensive index of statistics sources on the Web. Organized by topic area. The list is based on the publication, *Finding Statistics Online*, by Paula Berinstein. http://www.berinsteinresearch.com/stats.htm
	FedStats A gateway to statistical databases maintained by federal government agencies. http://www.fedstats.gov/ The "MapStats" section of this Web site generates county data profiles with agricultural, demographic, economic, crime, and environmental data. http://www.fedstats.gov/mapstats/
	Economic Statistics Briefing Room, The White House A user-friendly gateway to federal government economic statistics. http://www.whitehouse.gov/fsbr/esbr.html
	National Technical Information Service, U.S. Dept. of Commerce A gateway to U.S. federal government publications on business, environment, health, and military. http://www.ntis.gov/
	University of California, San Diego Contains a search engine of over 850 Internet sites of numeric social science statistical data. http://odwin.ucsd.edu/idata/
	U.S. Census Bureau, State Data Centers Contains a map of the 50 states with lists of Web sites in each state that provide access to U.S. Census data. http://www.census.gov/sdc/www/

GFOA Recommended Practice: Analysis of Debt Capacity

The Government Finance Officers Association (GFOA) recommends that governmental issuers issue debt prudently. A comprehensive, routine analysis of debt capacity provides assurance that the amount of debt is affordable and cost effective. When governments issue bonds, they enter into a long-term commitment that requires them to make timely principal and interest payments over the life of the bonds. Hence, they need to ensure that:

- Future debt service payments to bondholders can be made in full and on time without jeopardizing the provision of essential services,
- An acceptable degree of flexibility, including sufficient revenues, to meet unanticipated expenditures and accommodate revenue fluctuations is preserved,
- Outstanding debt obligations will not threaten long-term financial stability, and
- The amount of outstanding debt will not place undue burden on community residents and businesses.

Prior to issuing bonds, the GFOA recommends that governmental issuers undertake an analysis of their debt capacity. This analysis is intended to assess a government's long-term capacity to issue and repay debt. The debt capacity analysis helps to ensure that outstanding and planned debt does not exceed an amount that can be supported by the existing tax and revenue base. By analyzing debt capacity and establishing appropriate limits on debt issuance based on this analysis, governments are better able to keep debt at affordable levels.

An analysis of debt capacity should cover a broad range of factors. The following factors are recommended in evaluating debt capacity:

- Statutory or constitutional limitations affecting the amount that can be issued, including:
    —legally authorized debt limits, and
    —tax or expenditure ceilings;
- Other legal limitations, such as coverage requirements or additional bonds tests imposed by bond covenants;
- Measures of the tax and revenue base, such as:
    —projections of key, relevant economic variables (e.g., assessed property values, employment base, unemployment rates, income levels, and retail sales),
    —population trends,
    —utilization trends for services underlying revenues, and
    —factors affecting tax collections, including types of property, goods, or services taxed, assessment practices, and collection rates;
- Evaluation of trends relating to the government's financial performance, including:
    —revenues and expenditures,
    —net revenues available after meeting operating requirements,
    —reliability of revenues expected to pay debt service, and
    —unreserved fund balance levels;
- Debt service obligations, such as:
    —existing debt service requirements, and
    —debt service as a percentage of expenditures, or tax or system revenues;

- Measures of debt burden on the community, such as:
    —debt per capita,
    —debt as a percentage of personal income,
    —debt as a percentage of full or equalized assessed property value, and
    —overlapping or underlying debt; and
- Tax-exempt market factors affecting interest costs, including:
    —interest rates,
    —market receptivity, and
    —credit rating.

Governments should consider including a provision on debt limitations in their debt policy based on their analysis of debt capacity. This provides formal guidance to policy makers and government officials when making decisions on the amount of debt to issue. It also is essential for effective management of debt capacity that debt-planning activities be integrated with the capital improvement planning process. This ensures that an appropriate balance is struck between a jurisdiction's capital needs and its ability to pay for them.